InDesign CC - Beyond The Basics

A Step-By-Step Training Guide

InDesign is the desktop publishing industry standard used to develop marketing brochures and catalogs.

This manual provides the advanced features of Adobe InDesign to create and design content for the Web as well as print. There are over 60 unique character and paragraph formatting features. We will document all, and cover extensively, the most commonly used ones. Students will discover the "Library Feature" which will allow for the storage of images, logos, and text boxes for easy access. The "Books" feature will define each chapter as a separate file, and allow page numbers to be automatically adjusted. This will reduce the overall file size of the document by splitting it up into segments. The "Large Document" feature has the ability to use styles in order to create a Table of Contents, footnotes, and an index. The final project for the course will be a more creative process which will require using many of the manipulation and formatting capabilities taught in the class. Rather than giving a predefined layout, students will need to develop their own style based on the concepts covered. Commands are provided for **InDesign CC**, **CS6**, and **InDesign Mac CS6.**

Table of Contents

Student Projects

About the Author

Jeff Hutchinson is a computer instructor teaching a variety of classes around the country. He has a BS degree from BYU in Computer-Aided Engineering and has worked in the Information Technology field supporting and maintaining computers for many years. He also previously owned a computer training and consulting firm in San Francisco, California. After selling his business in 2001, he has continued to work as an independent computer instructor/consultant around the country. Jeff Hutchinson lives in Utah and also provides training for Utah Valley University Community Education system, offering valuable computer skills for the general knowledge of students, career development, and career advancement. Understanding the technology and the needs of students has been the basis for developing this material. Jeff Hutchinson can be contacted at jeffhutch@elearnlogic.com or (801) 376-6687.

Copyright and Release Information

ISBN-13: 978-1976467004 ISBN-10: 1976467004

Exercise Download

Exercises are posted on the website and can be downloaded to your computer.
Please do the following:

Open Internet Explorer/Edge:  Or Google Chrome: 

Type the web address:

elearnlogic.com/download/indesigncc-2.exe

You might get several security warnings, but answer yes and run through each one. When you click "**Unzip**," the files will be located in C:\Data\InDesignCC-2 folder.

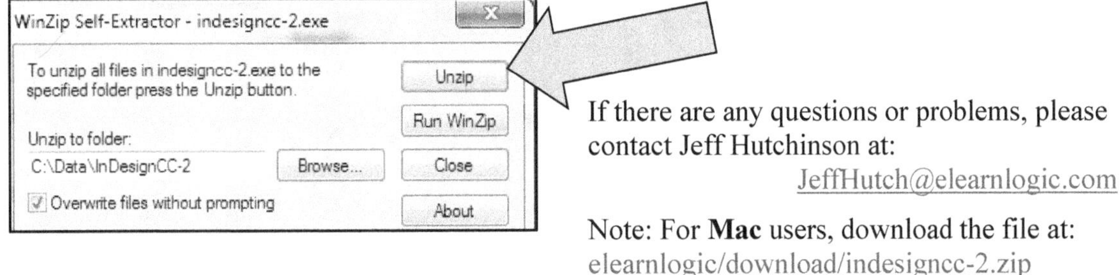

If there are any questions or problems, please contact Jeff Hutchinson at:
JeffHutch@elearnlogic.com

Note: For **Mac** users, download the file at:
elearnlogic/download/indesigncc-2.zip

Design Strategy

This workbook is designed in conjunction with an Online-Instructor-Led course (for more information see: www.elearnlogic.com). Unlike other computer guides, students will not need to review lengthy procedures in order to understand a topic. All that is necessary are the brief statements and command paths located within the guide that demonstrate how a concept is used. There are many **Step-By-Step Practice Exercises** and more comprehensive **Student Projects** used to better understand a concept. Furthermore, students will find that this workbook guide is often used as a reference to help users understand concepts quickly. An index is also provided on the last page of the workbook to reference important topics as necessary. However, if more detail is needed for study, the Internet can be used to search a concept. Also, if student's skills are weak due to lack of use, they can refresh their knowledge quickly by visually scanning the concept needed and then testing them out using the application.

Manual Organization

The following are special formatting conventions:

- **Numbered Sections** on the left are the **Concepts** covered.
- **Italic Text** is used to highlight commands that will perform the **Concept** or procedure in completing the practice exercises.
- **Practice Exercises** are a **Step-by-Step** approach to demonstrate the **Concept.**
- **Student Projects** are a more comprehensive approach to demonstrate the **Concept.**
- **Dark, Grayed-Out Sections** are optional/advanced **Concepts.**
- **Bolded** items are important **Concepts,** terminology or commands used.
- **Tip -** These are additional ideas about the **Concept.**

Chapter 1 - Fundamental Features Review

In this chapter, we will review the basic concepts necessary to reinforce the foundation of **InDesign**.

Concept	Explanation / *Command String in italic.*
1.1 Exercises	Exercise files on a **PC** are located at **C:\Data\InDesignCC-2** folder and the **Mac** files are usually stored on the desktop in the **InDesignCC-2** folder.
Practice Exercise 1	***File Menu→Open→*** **C:\Data\InDesignCC-2**. ***Brochure Excel Networks.indd***
1.2 Mac vs Windows	There are a few fundamental differences to identify: **Ctrl** key (used in MS Windows) = **command** key (used in Mac) **Alt** key (used in MS Windows) = **option** key (used in Mac) ***Edit Menu→Preferences*** *(used in MS Windows)* = ***InDesign→Preferences*** *(Mac)*
1.3 Panels	**Common panels used:** Color, Swatches, Gradient, Fills and Stroke, Alignment, Transform Objects, Links, and Effects Palette. ***Window Menu→ Choose panel.***
1.4 Story Editor	**This is used to edit the thread:** ***Edit Menu→Edit in Story Editor.*** **This turns on Red Underlines:** ***Edit Menu→Spelling→Dynamic Spelling.*** **This is used to add words to the dictionary:** ***Edit Menu→Spelling→Dictionary→Word: Testy→Add.*** Create a dictionary: ***Edit Menu→Preferences→Dictionary→ New Dictionary Icon*** Mac CS6: **InDesign Menu→Preferences→Dictionary.**
1.5 Tables	**Tables** are easy to use: ***Table Menu→Create, Insert, Delete,*** *and* ***Select.*** **InDesign CC:** The manipulation of **Tables** has been improved. Prior to version **InDesign CC**, you had to create a text box prior to inserting a **Table**: ***Type Tool→****Draw box****→Table Menu→Insert Table.***
1.6 Placement	**This is used for Graphics and Text.** ***File Menu→Place.***
1.7 Text Frames	**Frame Handles:** *Select text frame→move the round handles.*
1.7a Vertical Justification	**To adjust text vertically:** *Select text frame*→***Object Menu→Text Frame Options→****See the* ***Vertical Justification*** *Option.*
1.7b Inset Spacing	**This adjusts the text inside the frame:** *Select text frame*→***Object Menu→Text Frame Options→****See the* ***Inset Spacing.*** Test Test
1.8 Objects	**Stacking Order:** ***Object Menu→Arrange*, Concerting Shapes:** ***Object Menu→Convert Shape*, Fit a Frame**: ***Object Menu→Fitting*, Grouping Objects:** *Select Objects*→***Object Menu→Group***, and **Corner Options:** ***Object Menu→Corner Options.***
1.9 New Document	This includes facing Pages, Margins, Bleed, Slug, Pica, and Presets. ***File Menu→New→Document.***
1.10 Threading	**Manual, Simi-Automatic (Alt Key), Automatic (Shift Key), and Threads (View Menu→Extras→View Text Threads).**
1.11 Text Properties	**Text Wrap, Overset, Bullets, and Drop Cap.**
1.12 Master Pages	**Page Palette, Rename, Link Master, and Link to page.**

Chapter 2 - Object Adjustments

Here is a miscellaneous list of objects placed on a page.

Chapter Contents:

Section 1: Core Concepts

Concept	Explanation / *Command String in italic.*
2.1 Create Library	This is used to add frequently chosen objects: ***File Menu→New→Library.***
2.2 Add Objects to Library	Open the existing document, and drag/drop into library, Or Select ***Image→New Library*** *Item Button* . Note: Items added or removed from the library are automatically saved.
Practice Exercise 2 Library	Create a new library, add all items to the library. ***File Menu→Open→Exploring the Library.indd,*** ***File Menu→New→Library→C:\Data\InDesignCC-All\MyLibrary→Save.*** Use graphic images in a document in order to add to the library.
2.3 Link Panel	Objects placed have a link to the original location. However, the object is cashed in the active file. If the original file is changed, the link will allow the object to be updated. **=Original file is missing.** **=Original file was modified.**
Practice Exercise 3 Link	***File Menu→Place→Support.gif→Review Links Panel→Delete the physical file Support.gif→Review Links Panel →Rename SupportMod.gif to Support.gif→Review Links Panel →Select Support.gif →Click update Icon*** .
2.4 Color Bullets	***Type Tool→Select Text →More Options →Bullets and Numbering→Add new Bullet→Character Style: New Character Style.***
Practice Exercise 4 Bullet	***Type a list "Test1, Test2, Test3"→Select the list→More Options → Bullets and Numbering→List Type: Bullets→Add.***
2.5 Drag n Drop Copy	***Edit Menu→Preferences→Type→ Enable in Layout View.*** **Mac CS6: *InDesign Menu→Preferences.*** Note: Hold the **Alt** key down to copy the text box. **Mac CS6:** *Use Copy n Paste.*
Practice Exercise 5 Drag n Drop Copy	*Select Text box→Position pointer over the text box until you see the Drag n Drop Icon* ***→Hold the left mouse button and move text box to a new location.*** ***Mac CS6:*** *Look for a black cursor with the letter " T."*
2.6 Duplicate Items	Duplicate copy/paste. ***Select object→Alt Drag Object→Edit Menu→Duplicate*** or ***Select Object→Alt Drag→Edit Menu→Step/Repeat.*** ***Mac CS6: Select object→Hold Options Key→Drag n Drop→Edit Menu→Duplicate.***
2.7 Transparency	*Right-Click on Object* ***→Effects→Transparency→Opacity.*** **Mac CS6: *Object Menu→Effects.***
2.8 Clipping Paths	This removes the background of an image or allows the image to be transparent: ***File Menu→Place→Number5.jpg→Object Menu→Fitting→ Proportional.*** Note: The "**5**" won't fit in the frame because of the gray area. ***Select Number5.jpg→Object Menu→Clipping path→Options→Type: Detect Edges→Move threshold until gray area disappears.*** Type: Detect Edges OK Cancel Threshold: 162 Preview *also Try* Invert.

Practice Exercise 6 Clipping Path	***Try clipping Candle.jpg. Or, if you just want the image to be transparent, try clipping: OrigamiTriangle.tif.***
2.9 Compound Paths	***Window Menu→Object & Layout→Pathfinder.***
2.9a Join Path	This connects two end points. ***Draw 2 random lines→Hold the Shift Key down and click both lines to select them→ Join Path.***
2.9b Add	This combines selected objects into one shape. ***Draw 2 rectangles overlapping→ Add.***
2.9c Subtract	This subtracts the front objects from the back objects. ***Draw 2 rectangles overlapping→ Subtract.***
2.9d Intersect	This intersects the shape areas. ***Draw 2 rectangles overlapping→Intersect.***
2.9e Exclude Overlap	This excludes overlapping shape areas. ***Draw 2 rectangles overlapping→ Exclude Overlap.***
2.9f Minus Back	This subtracts the back objects from the front ones. ***Draw 2 rectangles overlapping→ Minus Back.***
Practice Exercise 7 Pathfinder	***Create a Bullet using Ellipse and Rectangle:*** ***Create a hole in the front of the bullet:***
2.10 Convert Paths	This converts to different shapes. ***Draw a square→Select object→ Convert to rectangle,*** **Rounded rectangle, Beveled rectangle, Inverse rounded rectangle, Ellipse, Triangle, Polygon, Line,** and Vertical/Horizontal Line) Note: You can also convert shapes using ***Object Menu→Convert Shape.***
Practice Exercise 8 Convert Shapes	***File Menu→Place→ "Olympic-Ladies Free Skate.jpg"→Window Menu→ Object and Layout→Pathfinder→Select image→Use one of the convert shapes.***
2.11 Type Outlines	This converts text to graphics: ***Text Box→Type: This is a custom font→Select Type→Type Menu→Create Outlines.***
2.12 Modification Date	This will insert the last date the document was modified. ***Type→Text Variables→Insert Variable→Modification Date.***
2.13 Move Connection Points	When using the **Pen Tool** on a rectangle, you can move the **Anchor Point.** *Draw a rectangle→Pen Tool→Hold Ctrl→Move the corner point to change the shape.* Note: When you hold the **Ctrl Key** down, look for the white square box under the cursor. Also, sometimes you may need to hold the **Ctrl Key** down and simultaneously click the line near the corner until the point turns white. . **Mac CS6:** *Hold **Command Key** to move the cursor.*
2.14 Distort a Rectangle	***Draw a rectangle→ + Add Anchor Point Tool→Add anchor point on the straight edge→Pen Tool→Hold Ctrl→Move the new anchor point to change the shape.*** **Mac CS6:** *Hold **Command Key**.*

Student Project A - Origami Exercise

This Origami drawing has some unique shape adjustment strategies that will give a different perspective to layouts.

1. ***File Tab→New→Document→X Facing Pages→Number of Pages: 3→Ok.***
2. ***Switch to page 2-3 facing pages.***
3. ***Create a Text box on the left side of the facing pages.***
   Create "History of", "O", and "rgami," three separate text boxes.
   To create an Octagon (8 edges), use 2 squares and rotate them. Also, group the squares.
4. ***File Tab→Place→ C:\Data\InDesignCC-All\Origami-Purple.tif***
5. ***File Tab→Place→C:\Data\InDesignCC-All\OrigamiText.docx.***
   Create 2 text boxes, one for each page.
   Use the Frame Options to add 2 columns to each page.
   Use the Direct Select tool to change the shape of the text box.
6. ***File Tab→Place→ C:\Data\InDesignCC-All\OrigamiTrangle.tif.***
   Use the Convert Shape to obtain the perfect triangle and use Direct Select to fit the object.
7. Create a square text box, copy it, and rotate the copy 90 degrees.
   Use the **Pen Tool** along with the **Ctrl** command to change the shape of the text box.
8. Add other shapes as shown in the example below:

Here are the text files to use:

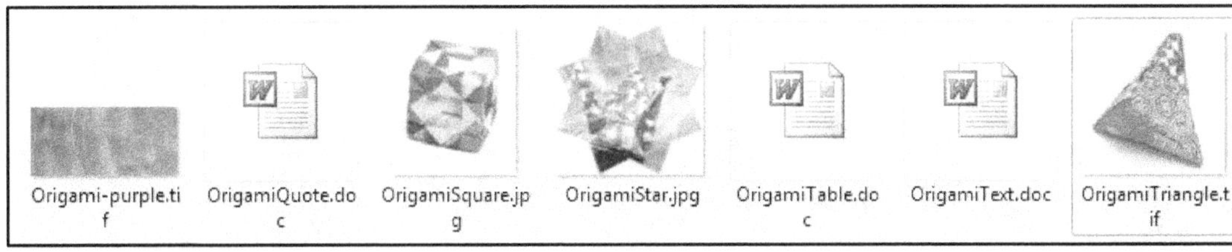

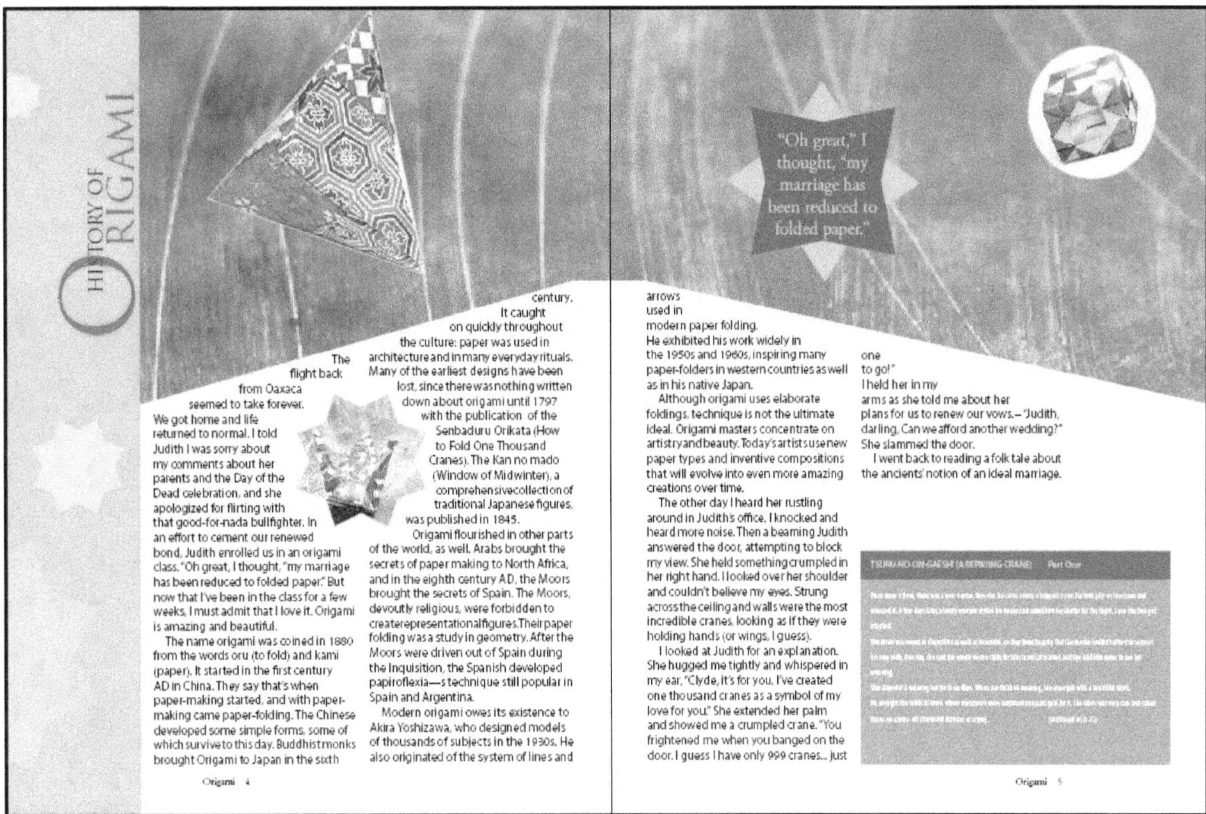

HISTORY OF ORIGAMI

"Oh great," I thought, "my marriage has been reduced to folded paper."

The flight back from Oaxaca seemed to take forever. We got home and life returned to normal. I told Judith I was sorry about my comments about her parents and the Day of the Dead celebration, and she apologized for flirting with that good-for-nada bullfighter. In an effort to cement our renewed bond, Judith enrolled us in an origami class. "Oh great, I thought, "my marriage has been reduced to folded paper." But now that I've been in the class for a few weeks, I must admit that I love it. Origami is amazing and beautiful.

The name origami was coined in 1880 from the words oru (to fold) and kami (paper). It started in the first century AD in China. They say that's when paper-making started, and with paper-making came paper-folding. The Chinese developed some simple forms, some of which survive to this day. Buddhist monks brought Origami to Japan in the sixth century. It caught on quickly throughout the culture: paper was used in architecture and in many everyday rituals. Many of the earliest designs have been lost, since there was nothing written down about origami until 1797 with the publication of the Senbaduru Orikata (How to Fold One Thousand Cranes). The Kan no mado (Window of Midwinter), a comprehensive collection of traditional Japanese figures, was published in 1845.

Origami flourished in other parts of the world, as well. Arabs brought the secrets of paper making to North Africa, and in the eighth century AD, the Moors brought the secrets of Spain. The Moors, devoutly religious, were forbidden to create representational figures. Their paper folding was a study in geometry. After the Moors were driven out of Spain during the Inquisition, the Spanish developed papiroflexia—s technique still popular in Spain and Argentina.

Modern origami owes its existence to Akira Yoshizawa, who designed models of thousands of subjects in the 1930s. He also originated of the system of lines and

Origami 4

arrows used in modern paper folding. He exhibited his work widely in the 1950s and 1960s, inspiring many paper-folders in western countries as well as in his native Japan.

Although origami uses elaborate foldings, technique is not the ultimate ideal. Origami masters concentrate on artistry and beauty. Today's artists use new paper types and inventive compositions that will evolve into even more amazing creations over time.

The other day I heard her rustling around in Judith's office. I knocked and heard more noise. Then a beaming Judith answered the door, attempting to block my view. She held something crumpled in her right hand. I looked over her shoulder and couldn't believe my eyes. Strung across the ceiling and walls were the most incredible cranes, looking as if they were holding hands (or wings, I guess).

I looked at Judith for an explanation. She hugged me tightly and whispered in my ear, "Clyde, it's for you. I've created one thousand cranes as a symbol of my love for you." She extended her palm and showed me a crumpled crane. "You frightened me when you banged on the door. I guess I have only 999 cranes... just one to go!"

I held her in my arms as she told me about her plans for us to renew our vows.– "Judith, darling, Can we afford another wedding?" She slammed the door.

I went back to reading a folk tale about the ancients' notion of an ideal marriage.

TSURU-NO-ON-GAESHI (A REPAYING CRANE) Part One

Origami 5

The completed version is called: **C:\Data\InDesignCC-1\Origami Finished.indd**

Section 2: Optional Concepts

Concept	Explanation / *Command String in italic.*
2.15 Static Captions	This is a caption that appears under the image. ***Select Object→Object Menu→Captions→Generate static Caption.***
Practice Exercise 9 Static Caption	***File Menu→Place→ Olympic-Sasha.jpg→Select the image→ Object Menu→ Caption→Generate Static Caption.***
2.16 Live Captions	When you move a caption to a new image, the file name in the caption adjusts to the new image. ***File Menu→Place→Image1. File Menu→Place→Image2, Right-Click on Image→Caption→Live Caption→Select Tool→Move Caption to new Image.***
Practice Exercise 10 Live Caption	***File Menu→Place→B-House1.jpg, B-House2.jpg, B-House3.jpg →Select B-House1.jpg→Object Menu→Caption→ Generate Live Caption→Select B-House1.jpg caption→Move and drop on top of B-House2.jpg.***
2.17 Anchored Objects	**Anchored Objects** InLine - This works the same as if you placed a graphic image next to a text string. The advantage is that you can adjust its position within the line. ***Type Tool→Draw Box→Type text→Place Cursor in text→Object Menu→ Anchored Object→Insert→Content: Graphic.***
Practice Exercise 11 Anchored Objects	***File Menu→Place→"Anchored InLine Graphic.docx"→ Font Size: 30. Place Cursor in text→Object Menu→Anchored Object→Insert→Content: Graphic.*** *Complete the options below:* Insert Anchored Object Object Options Content: Graphic Object Style: [Basic Graphics Frame] Paragraph Style: [No Paragraph Style] Height: 1p0 Width: 1p0 Position: Inline or Above Line Inline Y Offset: 0p0 This is an Anchored InLine Graphic. A graphic image can be placed within a line. **To Place a Graphic image in the graphic frame:** ***Select Tool →Select or highlight the anchor object→File Menu→Place→Logo.jpg→ Object Menu→ Fitting→Fit Frame Proportionally.***
2.18 Anchored Objects Inline	Place a graphic in the middle of the text. Example: This ▮ is a test. ***Place graphic in a text string→Select Graphic→Object Menu→Anchored Object Options→Position: Inline or Above Line.*** ***Inline Y Offset - 1P.***
2.19 Anchored Objects Above	This inserts a graphic frame that is tied to the line. When you move the text box, the graphic image will stay tied together. After you create the **Anchored object**, select the image frame and insert a graphic image. ***Place Cursor in text→ Object Menu →Anchored Object→Insert→Content: Graphic.***

Practice Exercise 12 Anchored Objects Above Line	***File Menu→Place→Anchored InLine Graphic.docx→Font Size: 30.*** ***Place Cursor in text→Object Menu→Anchored Object→Insert→Content: Graphic*** *Complete the options below:* 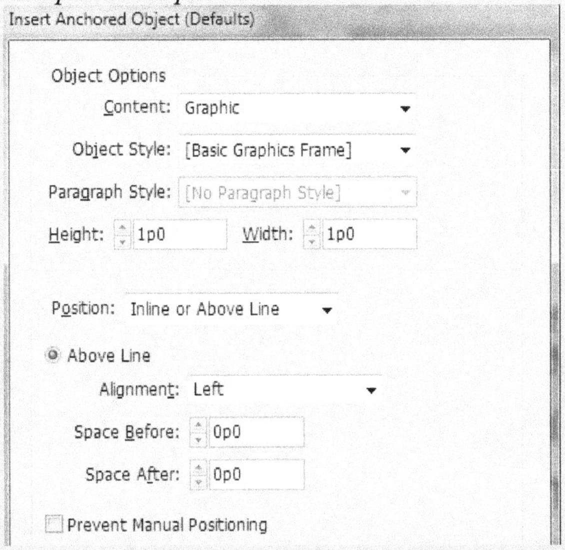 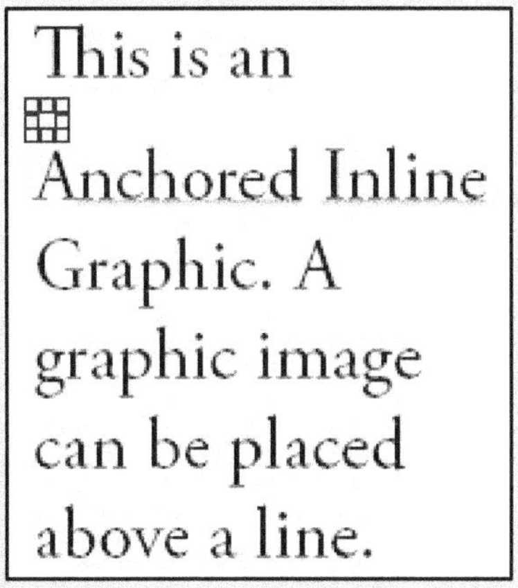 Insert Anchored Object (Defaults) Object Options Content: Graphic Object Style: [Basic Graphics Frame] Paragraph Style: [No Paragraph Style] Height: 1p0 Width: 1p0 Position: Inline or Above Line Above Line Alignment: Left Space Before: 0p0 Space After: 0p0 Prevent Manual Positioning This is an Anchored Inline Graphic. A graphic image can be placed above a line. To change the position: ***Select the graphic object→Object Menu→Anchored Object→Options→ Above Line→Alignment: Center***
2.20 Bookmark	A bookmark is an Acrobat PDF feature that can be added within InDesign. Once added, bookmarks will be available in Acrobat when converted. 1. ***Window Menu→Interactive→Bookmarks**, **Select Text→Right-Click→ Interactive→New Bookmark.*** 2. ***File Menu→Export→Adobe PDF Print→*** Bookmarks ***→Export.*** 3. ***Open PDF file and preview the bookmarks on the left side of the screen.*** **Mac CS6:** *Select text→Bookmarks more options* ***→New Bookmark.***
2.21 Interactive Buttons	This allows you to create an action on the buttons: Place the ArrowLeft.gif on the master page. ***Select ArrowLeft.gif→ Object Menu→Interactive→Convert to*** *Button*→ + ***→Go to Previous Page***.

Chapter 3 - Tools Panel

All the tools located on the left side of the screen will be covered in this chapter.

1	2
3	4
5	6
7	8
9	10
11	12
13	14
15	16
17	18
19	20
21	
22	23
24,25	26
27	28

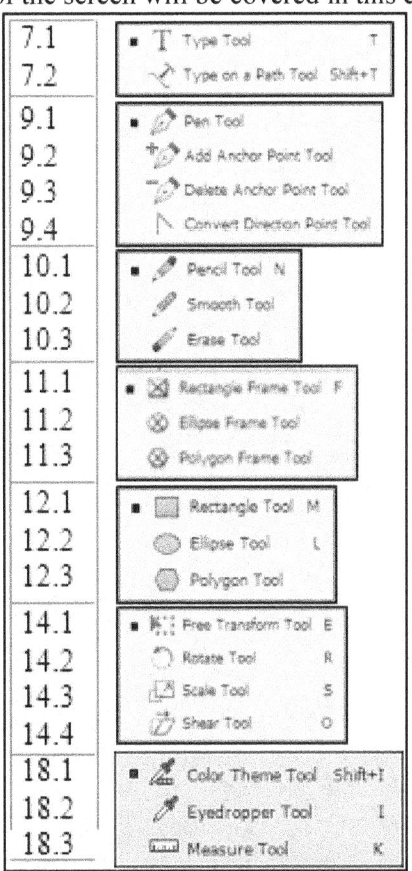

1 - Selection Tool	This selects and manipulates a frame.
2 - Direct Selection Tool	This manipulates the graphic within a frame. The bulls' eye circle in the middle of an object will switch to the Direct Select **Tool**.
3 - Page Tool	This changes the page size. It may be different from the default page size. To adjust the page, hold the ***Alt Key*** down when moving the page tags located on each corner and side of the page.
Practice Exercise 13 Page Tool	*Create a ½ page fold-out: **File Menu →New →Document →** **Facing Pages, Number of Pages: 3 →Ok.** **Page Tool →Select page 3 →Hold the Alt button and size the page by selecting the right side.*** *Click just inside the page marker and drag in the word.*
4 - Gap Tool	This adjusts gaps between frames. ***Place 2 images →Gap Tool →Change gap distance.***
5 - Content Collector Tool	This is a temporary storage used to place text boxes and images. It does not save along with the document. The **InDesign CS6+** feature is similar to the **Library** feature. You can place objects on the **Content Conveyor**.
6 - Content Placer Tool	The CS6+ Feature pulls objects out of the content conveyor and places them in a new document.

Practice Exercise 14 Content Collector/Placer	***File Menu→Place→ B-House1.jpg, B-Houst2.jpg→Content Collector Tool→Click on the images to put them in the Content Conveyer→Open a new document→Content Placer Tool→****Place the images in the new document.*
Practice Exercise 15 Linking text Using the Content Tools	***File Menu→New→Document→****create text box→Test1→* ***Content Collector Tool→Place text box in the Content Conveyer→Content Placer Tool→*** Create Link ***→Place text box→You will see a chain link on top→Modify text box 1→you will see on text box2→Click to update link.***
7.1 - Type Tool	This is used to enter text. Three options will be available: 1) **Formatting** 2) **Paragraph** 3) **More formatting** options.
7.2 - Type on a Path Tool	You can attach the text to drawing tool such as **Ellipse**, angle, or use the **Pen Tools**. ***Pen Tool→Draw Curve→Text on Path Tool→Select path→type text.***
Practice Exercise 16 Type on Ellipse	***Draw Ellipse→Type on a Path Tool→Look for the cursor to change to an I+→Type around the Ellipse.***
8.1 - Line Tool	This simply draws **Lines**. Holding the ***Shift Key*** will draw the line in 90° increments. Holding the ***Alt Key*** will draw from the center out.
9 - Pen Tools	This allows you to add or remove anchor points to create curved or straight lines. The + and - tools are not needed because they are built into the **Pen Tool**.
9.1 - Pen Tool	***Pen Tool→****Click point A and release the left mouse button→Click point B and don't let go of left mouse button→Move the point around to draw an arc.*
9.2 - +Anchor Point	This adds an anchor point to a line segment.
9.3 - -Anchor Point	This subtracts an anchor point on a line segment.
Practice Exercise 17 Pen Tool	***File Menu→Place→3D Cup.jpg→Create a label for your coffee cup using the Pen tools similar to:*** My Coffee Cup
9.4 - Convert Shape	While you are using the Pen **Tool**, hold the **Alt Key** *(**Mac CS6:** Use the **Options Key**)* to drop into the Covert Shape. ***Pen Tool→Click→Click→Click→ Chick→Click→Hold the Alt Key*** *(**Mac CS6:** Use the **Options Key**)* ***→Move the anchor point.***
10.1 - Pencil Tool	This draws free hand. Using the **Alt Key** *(**Mac CS6:** Use the **Options Key**)* will allow you to shift into the **Smooth Tool**.
10.2 - Smooth Tool	This progressively smooths out jagged edges.
10.3 - Erase Tool	This **Erases** or deletes a path segment. In order to **Erase** an object, the anchor points must be visible.
Practice Exercise 18 Pencil Tool	*Draw straight lines using the* ***Pencil Tool→Use the Smooth Tool to flatten the points→Test the Eraser Tool.***
11.1 - Rectangle Frame Tool	This is used as a placeholder for graphic images. Holding the ***Shift Key*** will draw a perfect square. Holding the ***Alt Key*** will draw from the center out.
11.2 - Ellipse Frame Tool	This is used for text frames. Holding the ***Shift Key*** will draw a perfect circle. Holding the ***Alt Key*** will draw from the center out.
11.3 - Polygon Frame Tool	This is used for text frames. Holding the ***Shift Key*** will draw a perfect polygon. Holding the ***Alt Key*** will draw from the center out.
Practice Exercise 19 Frame	***Place a Rectangle Frame Tool in a new document→Select the frame→ File Menu→ Place→B-House3.jpg.***

12.1 - Rectangle Tool	This draws a rectangle and the **Shift Key** will draw a square. Holding the ***Alt Key*** will draw from the center out.
12.2 - Ellipse Tool	This draws an Ellipse and the **Shift Key** will draw a Circle. Holding the ***Alt Key*** will draw from the center out.
12.3 - Polygon Tool	This draws a polygon shape. Holding the ***Shift Key*** will draw a perfect polygon. Holding the ***Alt Key*** will draw from the center out.
*Practice Exercise 20 Rectangle **Tool***	*Draw a rectangle using 1)**Shift Key** 2)**Alt Key**(**Mac CS6:** Use the **Options Key**) 3)**Shift** and **Alt Keys**.*
13 - Scissors Tool	This cuts objects. Use the **Pin Tool** to add **Anchor Points** to cut.
Practice Exercise 21 Scissors	***File Menu→Place→B-House1.jpg→ Scissors Tool→Click on the top edge of the image→Click on the lower edge of the image→Select Tool→Move the images apart.***
14.1 - Free Transform Tool	This allows you to scale, and rotate objects. Operational in CS3+.
14.2 - Rotate Tool	This rotates objects. It is operational in CS3+.
14.3 - Scale Tool	This scales objects and is operational in CS3+.
14.4 - Shear Tool	This shears objects but is not operational in CS3+.
Practice Exercise 22 Manipulate Image	***File Menu→Place→ B-House2.jpg→Use the Free Transform, Rotate, Scale, and Shear Tools to manipulate the image).*** *Note: Test using the **Shift**, **Alt**, and **Shift/Alt Keys**.*
15 - Gradient Swatch Tool	This grades color from light to dark.
Practice Exercise 23 Color Gradient Swatch	***File Menu→New→Document→Rectangle Tool→Draw a Rectangle→Select the rectangle.*** ***Swatches Panel→More Options*** ***→New Gradient Swatch***. 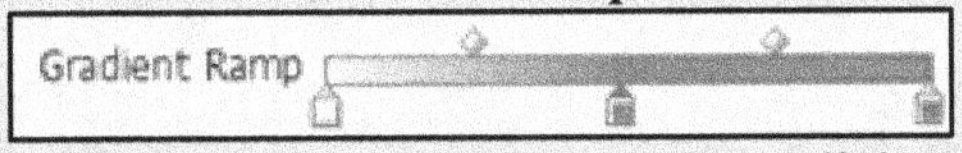 Gradient Ramp To add additional gradient colors, click under the **Gradient Ramp** (Stop Box). To change the gradient color, click on the square box (Stop box) and change the color. 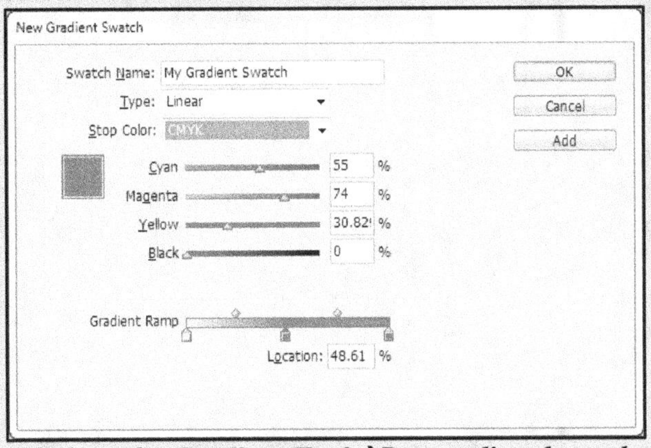 New Gradient Swatch Swatch Name: My Gradient Swatch Type: Linear Stop Color: CMYK Cyan 55 % Magenta 74 % Yellow 30.82! % Black 0 % Gradient Ramp Location: 48.61 % OK Cancel Add *Click on the **Gradient Tool→Draw a line through the new rectangle to change the color range of the Gradient Swatch**.*
16 - Gradient Feather Tool	This feathers a graphic image. The **Feather** will make the **Gradient** fuzzier between transitions.
Practice Exercise 24 Gradient Feather	***File Menu→Place→Any Image→Gradient Feather Tool→*** *1) Draw a line from the beginning of the object to the end of the object 2) Draw a line starting outside of the image and finish the line on the other side of the image.*

17 - Note Tool	This adds an editorial note to a text box. It can be used to add additional comments about the entered text. The note boxes do not print, however. In order to add a note to a graphic, you will need to add a caption, and then add the note. This is operational in CS3+.
18.1 - Eye Dropper Tool	Sample colors.
Practice Exercise 25 Eye Dropper Graphic Image	***File Menu→Place→Balos Beach Greece.jpg→Eye Dropper Tool→Sample the Sky→View the Color Panel in the lower left corner→*** .
Practice Exercise 26 Eye Dropper Text Format	***File Menu→Place→ Anchored InLine Graphic.docx→Format the word "Anchored" to be Bold→Eye Dropper Tool→Sample the word "Anchored" → Paint the word Graphic using the Eye Dropper.***
18.2 -Measurement Tool	This measures distance and is operational in CS3+.
19 - Hand Tool	This adjusts a page and moves the entire page.
20 - Zoom Tool	This draws a box around the area.
21 - Color Fill	This fills an object with a specified color.
22 - Formatting Effects Container	When you select 2 or more objects, it changes the fill (**Swatches Panel**) and border (**Stroke Panel**) at the same time.
23 - Formatting Effects text	**T** When you select 2 or more text boxes, it changes the font color of both text boxes at the same time.
Practice Exercise 27 Formatting Effects	1. Create several text boxes: ***Text box1→Test1→Font: Arial→Text box2→ Test2→Font: Times New Roman.*** 2. ***Select text box1→Shift→Select text box2→Formatting Effects Container button →Swatches Panel→Yellow Fill→ Formatting Effects Text button* T**. 3. ***Type Tool→Change the format to Blackoak Std.***
24, 25, 26 - Apply Color, Gradient, and None.	
27 - Normal Display	This is the normal working view.
28 - Preview View	Preview the document without guides, borders, frames, etc.
28 - Bleed View	Preview the bleed area which includes the graphic objects.
28 - Slug View	Preview the slug area which includes labels/identification.
28 - Presentation View	Preview the layout in the presentation mode.

Student Project B - Using the Tools

Step 1 - Create a new document: ***File Menu→New→Document,*** Landscape, Margin: .5 in (3p0), 2 columns.

Step 2 - Create 3 frame boxes using the **Rectangle Frame Tool** and place the following files:

Hawaii - Black Sand Beach.docx
Hawaii - Polihale Beach.docx
Hawaii - Wailea Beach.docx.

Step 3 - Select the frame and place the following images:

Hawaii - Black Sand Beach.jpg
Hawaii - Polihale Beach.jpg
Hawaii - Wailea Beach.jpg.

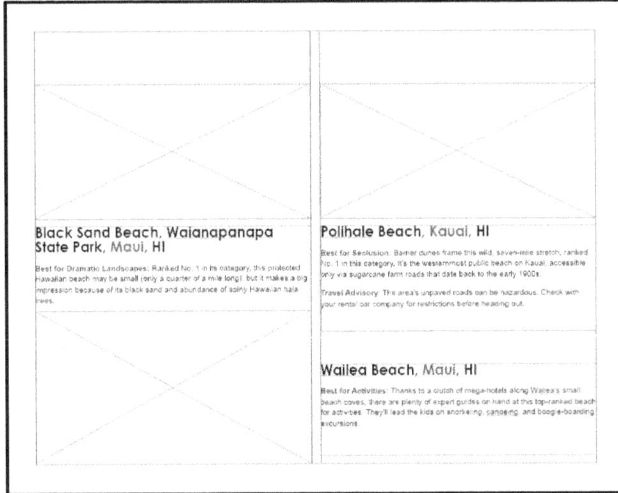

Step 4 - Use the Select and **Direct Select Tool** to adjust the images.
Step 5 - Use the **Type on a Path Tool** to curve the title. Use the **Pen Tool** to create a curved path. Use the **Type on a Path Tool** to enter the following text: Hawaiian Beaches.
Step 6 - Adjust images: Use the **Free Transform Tool** to rotate an image. Use the **Shear Tool** to shear an image.
Step 7 - Format the font size and use the **Eye Dropper Tool** to format the other text paragraphs.
Step 8 - Use this document to test any of the tools above.

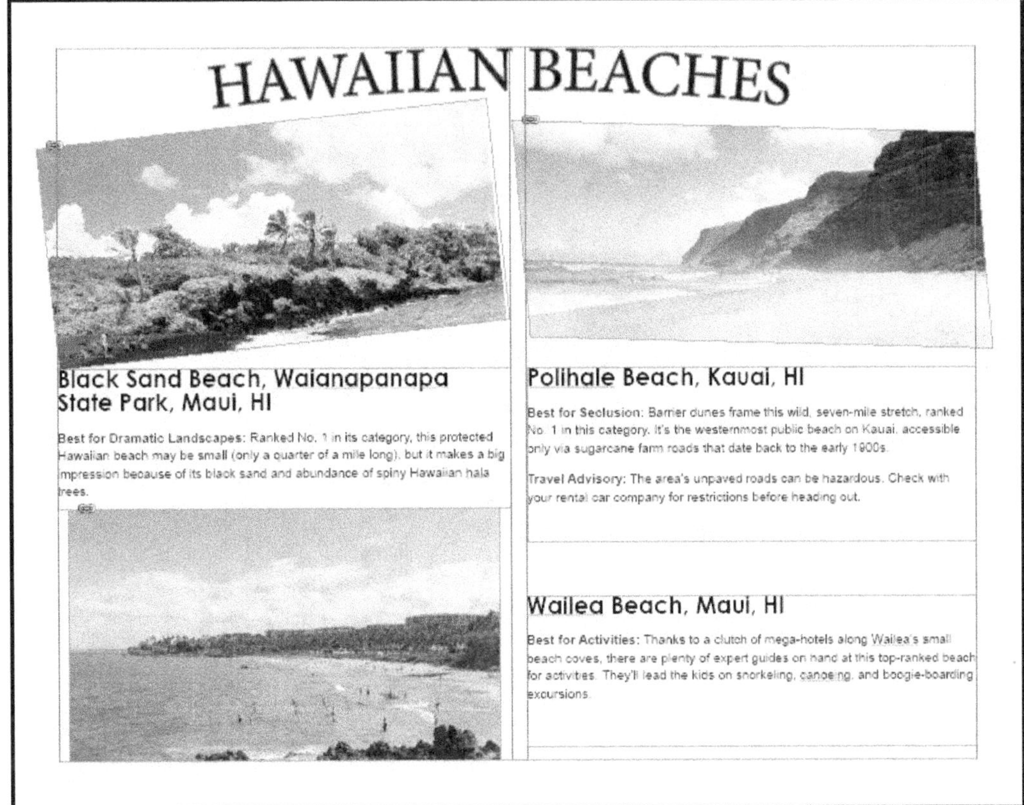

The completed version is called: Hawaii1.Indd, Hawaii2.Indd, and Hawaii3.Indd.

Chapter 4 - Formatting

This chapter covers all character and paragraph formatting options. The concepts in **bold** are the most commonly used, but all are covered to provide a comprehensive review.

To set the default font, size and type: Open **InDesign** and make sure all documents are closed (**Very Important!**). ***Window Menu→Type&Table→Character***. Make the necessary changes. **Test It:** ***File Menu→New→Document→Ok→Type Tool→***(The default should be set). Close **InDesign** and reopen it to test it again.

Chapter Contents:

Section 1: Character Formatting Control Panel

1 3 5 7 9 11 13 15 17 19 21 22

2 4 6 8 10 12 14 16 18 20

Character Formatting	
1 - Character Formatting Controls	When you choose the **Type Tool**, the top changes to the character format controls. Click on this symbol to switch to the **Character Formatting** controls.
2 - Paragraph Formatting Controls	When you click on the **Paragraph** button ¶, the top changes to the paragraph control.
3 - Font Family	Font examples are **Arial, Times New Roman**, etc.
4 - Character Type	Character type examples are **Regular, Italic, Bold, Bold Italic.**
5 - Font Size	The value can be typed in, or chosen from the pull-down menu.
6 - Leading	This adjusts the spacing between words on two rows. ***W1→Enter Key→W2→Select both→Change the Leading value.***
7 - All Caps	This converts selected text to **Caps**.
8 - Small Caps	This converts selected text too small letters.
9 - Superscript	This converts selected text to superscript or offsets the text above such as a power symbol. ***Type 52→Select 2→Click Superscript button.***
10 - Subscript	This places the text down or offset from the center such as a Log of 2. ***Type Log2→Select 2→Click Subscript button.***
11 - Underline	This adds an **underline** to the selected text.
12 - Strikethrough	This puts a **line through** selected text.
13 - Kerning	This will adjust a specified **distance between characters** that overlap. For example, WA can be kerned so the W and A fit closer together. This is used to better fit a title on a line by bringing all character's closer together. To turn it off: choose 0. Some common kerning examples are: **LA, P., To, Tr, Ta, Tu, Te, Ty, Wa, WA, We, Wo, Ya, and Yo.**
Practice Exercise 28 Kerning	***Type WA→Change font size to 72 pts→Place the cursor between the text W|A→Change kerning to -50.***
13a - Kerning Metrics	This depends on **Kern pairs AP, AF, AT, FA, LV, and LW.** **Metric Kerning** is included in most fonts.
13b - Kerning Optical	This is useful for characters with different font types. When using different type faces or sizes, **Optical Kerning** is best.
14 - Tracking	This loosens or tightens a block of text, but will not affect the **Kerning.**

Practice Exercise 29 Tracking	*Type: **WA→Change font size to 72 pts→Select both letters WA→Change Tracking to -50.***
15 - Vertical Scale	The scales select larger or smaller text in a **vertical** direction.
Practice Exercise 30 Vertical Scale	*Type the word: **TEST→Select the text→Change the vertical scale value.***
16 - Baseline Shift	You can move a selected character up or down a specific distance from the baseline. (**2nd** shifts upward and **Log$_{23}$** shifts downward**).**
Practice Exercise 31 Baseline Shift	***Type the word: Log23→Select 23→change the baseline shift value.***
17 - Horizontal Scale	The scales select larger or smaller text in a horizontal direction.
Practice Exercise 32 Horizontal Scale	***Type the word: TEST→Select the text→Change the horizontal scale value.***
18 - Skew	This **angles the text** similar to italic formatting. Positive numbers slant the top of the text to the right, and negative numbers slant the top of the text to the left.
19 - Character Style	A **character style** name can have preformatted character attributes applied to it. (See the styles chapter below).
20 - Language	Usually English: USA
21 - Quick Apply	This **quickly applies** a style.
22 - Character Menu	These are additional character formatting options. (See the **Character Formatting** section below).

Section 2: Paragraph Formatting Control Panel

1 3 5 7 9 11 13 15 17 19 21 23 25 27 28

2 4 6 8 10 12 14 16 18 20 22 24 26

1 - Character Formatting Controls	Switch back to the **character formatting controls.**
2 - Paragraph Formatting Controls	Click on this symbol ¶ to switch to the **Paragraph Formatting** controls.
3 - Left Align	The entire paragraph is **aligned to the left.**
4 - Justify with last line aligned left	Here, only the last line is affected.
5 - Center Align	The entire paragraph is **aligned to the center**.
6 - Justify with last line aligned center	Here, only the last line is affected.
7 - Right Align	The entire paragraph is **aligned to the right**.
8 - Justify all lines	This pushes all text on the **left to the margin**, and text on the right is pushed to the right margin.
9 - Align towards spine	The spine is the **center of facing pages**. Text in a paragraph on the left-hand page is right aligned. However, when the same text flows into the right-hand page, it becomes left aligned.
10 - Align away from spine	The spine is the **center of facing pages**. Text in a paragraph on the left-hand page is left aligned. However, when the same text flows into the right-hand page, it becomes right aligned.

11 - Left Indent	This indents a paragraph by a specific amount on the left which affects the entire paragraph.
12 - First line left indent	Only the first line is affected.
13 - Right Indent	This indents a paragraph by a specific amount on the right which affects the entire paragraph.
14 - Last line right indent	Only the last line is affected.
15 - Space Before	These are spaces placed before paragraphs by a certain specified amount.
16 - Drop Cap Number of Lines	This makes the **first letter larger** by a specified number of lines.
17 - Space After	These are spaces placed after a paragraph by a specified amount.
18 - Drop Cap one or more characters	This specifies the number of **Drop Cap characters** to be affected. ***Type text→Format options.***
19 - Bulleted List	This puts a bulleted list in front of the selected text.
20 - Numbered List	This puts a numbered list in front of the selected text.
21 - Paragraph Style	This is a style name that contains pre-formatted paragraph attributes.
22 - Hyphenate	This turns on the ability to continue a word on the next line. Example: think-ing.
23 - Do not align to baseline grid	Click to keep the paragraph text from aligning to the baseline grid.
24 - Clear Overrides in selection	This changes the local formatting in the selection to the underlying paragraph style.
25 - Number of columns	This splits a frame into a specified number of columns.
26 - Align to baseline grid	The **baseline grid** represents the leading for the body text in a document. You can use multiples of this leading value for all elements of the page to ensure that text always lines up between columns and from page to page. For example, if the body text in your document has 12-point leading, you could give your heading text 18-point leading and add 6 points of space before the paragraphs that follow the headings.
27 - Quick Apply	This quickly applies a style.
28 - More Options	There are additional paragraph formatting options available.

Section 3: More Character and Paragraph Options

1		OpenType ▸	
2	✓	Ligatures	
3		Underline Options....	
4		Strikethrough Options...	
5		No Break	
6		Adobe World-Ready Single-line Composer	
7		Adobe World-Ready Paragraph Composer	
8	✓	Adobe Paragraph Composer	
9		Adobe Single-line Composer	
10		Only Align First Line to Grid	
11		Balance Ragged Lines	
12		Ignore Optical Margin	
13		Justification...	Alt+Shift+Ctrl+J
14		Keep Options...	Alt+Ctrl+K
15		Span Columns...	
16		Hyphenation...	
17		Drop Caps and Nested Styles...	Alt+Ctrl+R
18		GREP Styles...	
19		Paragraph Rules...	Alt+Ctrl+J
20		Bullets and Numbering...	
21	✓	Dock at Top	
22		Dock at Bottom	
23		Float	
24		Customize...	

1 - OpenType	This contains many characters not available in other font types (such as fractions, small caps, superscript, subscript, and more).
2 - Ligatures	These are typographic replacement characters for certain letter pairs such as "fi" and "fl."
3 - Underline Options	This opens a dialog box with many different styles, weights, offsets, and colors available.
4 - Strikethrough Options	This opens a dialog box with many different styles, weights, offsets, and colors available.
5 - No Break	Select either a line, paragraph, column, or page and InDesign will refuse to allow a break to occur in any way.
6 - Adobe World-Ready Single-line Composer	This will adjust the text to look smoother or easier to read. ***Menu*** ▾≡ ***→Adobe World-Ready Single-line Composer***.
7 - Adobe World-Ready Paragraph Composer	This will adjust the paragraph to look smoother or easier to read. ***Menu*** ▾≡ ***→Adobe World-Ready Paragraph Composer.***
8 - Adobe Paragraph Composer	This determines the best line breaks and optimal word spacing of your paragraphs. ***Menu*** ▾≡ ***→Adobe Paragraph Composer.***
9 - Adobe Single-line Composer	This determines the best line breaks & optimal word spacing. ***Menu*** ▾≡ ***→Adobe Single-line Composer.***

10 - Only Align First Line to Grid	This will allow the first line of a text frame to align to the grid. The rest will be offset from the grid.
11 - Balance Ragged Lines	This is useful for preventing unequal line lengths in heading and subheadings. This attempts to adjust lines so the length of the lines are as close as possible to the same length. This is normally set up in paragraph styles.
12 - Ignore Optical Margin	This balances the edges of the columns based on the appearance of *all* the characters at the beginning or end of the lines in the column. ***Type the text on the right→Select Text→ Window Menu→Type&Tables→Story Panel.*** "S W "S W Story ☑ Optical Margin Alignment 12 pt Story ☐ Optical Margin Alignment 12 pt
13 - Justification	This refers to the **straight edges of a paragraph**. The feature loads the justification dialog box to fine-tune the word and letter spacing.
14 - Keep Options	This **keeps widows and orphans together**. **Widows** are a single line or title on top of a column. If it ends up on a page by itself, it will be forced into the main document. Orphans are a single line at the bottom of a column. This option will force two lines to stay together if the line appears on a separate page.
15 - Span Column	This is used to span or split columns of a paragraph.
16 - Hyphenation	This is a **dash at the end of a sentence**. The **Hyphenation** dialog box will adjust the parameters to allow a dash if the word extends beyond the line.
17 - Drop Caps and nested Styles	This creates a drop cap and provides additional style options.
18 - GREP Styles	This creates a **custom character style.**
19 - Paragraph Rules	This will add additional information to a paragraph.
Practice Exercise 33 Paragraph Rules	***Select a title→Menu options ▾≡ →Paragraph Rule→Rule Below→ ✓ Rule On→Weight: 5.***
20 - Bullets and Numbering	This allows you to choose the **bullet** and **number type.**
21 - Dock at top	This docks the Control panel on the **top of the screen**.
22 - Dock at bottom	This docks the Control panel on the **bottom of the screen**.
23 - Float	This allows the Control panel to **float.**
24 - Customize	This turns off features in the **Type options Menu.**

Student Project C - Text and Paragraph Options

Step 1 - Create a new document: ***File Menu→New→Document→ Portrait, 1 column, Margin: .5 in (3p0)→Ok.***

Step 2 - Place text: ***File Menu→Place→ D3-Restaurants.docx***

Step 3 - Character formatting: **Select all the text (5 clicks)→Font size: 9 pt→Leading: 12 pt.**

Select the first title→Size: 18 pt→Bold→Tracking: 30→Baseline Shift: 3 pt→ Use the Eye Dropper to format the other titles to be the same.

Step 4 - Paragraph formatting: **Select the first title→Center the title Overview**

Select all the text (5 clicks)→Space before: 0p3→Turn off Hyphenate ☐ Hyphenate .

Create a Drop Cap of 2 for the first paragraph 2

Create a custom **bulleted list** **(go to the end of the document on page 2.**

Change the bullet style: More Options →Bullets and Numbering→Add→Ok→ Select new character→Ok.

Step 5 - Use this document to test out any other formatting feature.

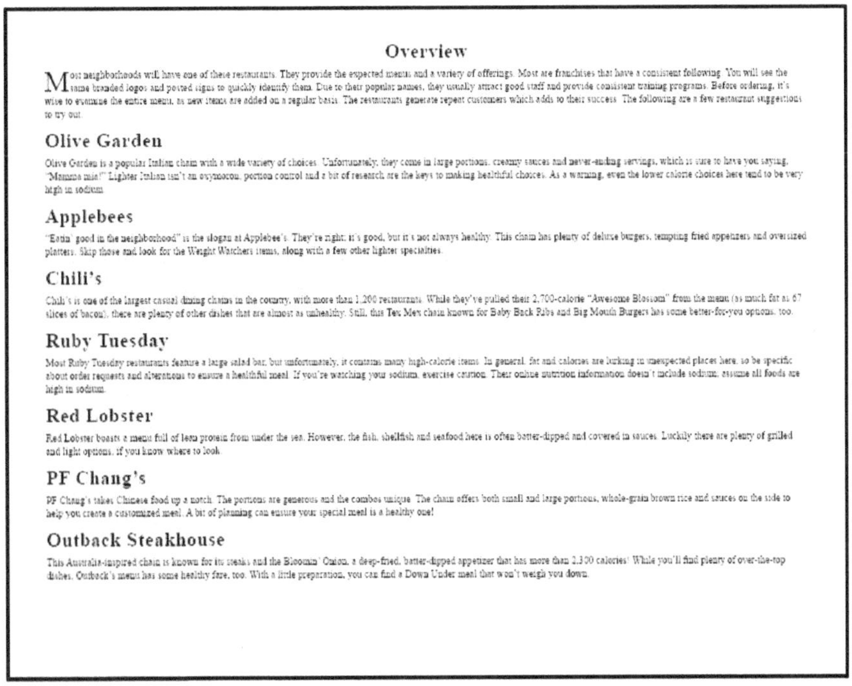

Overview

Most neighborhoods will have one of these restaurants. They provide the expected menus and a variety of offerings. Most are franchises that have a consistent following. You will see the same branded logos and posted signs to quickly identify them. Due to their popular names, they usually attract good staff and provide consistent training programs. Before ordering, it's wise to examine the entire menu, as new items are added on a regular basis. The restaurants generate repeat customers which adds to their success. The following are a few restaurant suggestions to try out.

Olive Garden

Olive Garden is a popular Italian chain with a wide variety of choices. Unfortunately, they come in large portions, creamy sauces and never-ending servings, which is sure to have you saying, "Mamma mia!" Lighter Italian isn't an oxymoron, portion control and a bit of research are the keys to making healthful choices. As a warning, even the lower calorie choices here tend to be very high in sodium.

Applebees

"Eatin' good in the neighborhood" is the slogan at Applebee's. They're right: it's good, but it's not always healthy. This chain has plenty of deluxe burgers, tempting fried appetizers and oversized platters. Skip those and look for the Weight Watchers items, along with a few other lighter specialties.

Chili's

Chili's is one of the largest casual dining chains in the country, with more than 1,200 restaurants. While they've pulled their 2,700-calorie "Awesome Blossom" from the menu (as much fat as 67 slices of bacon), there are plenty of other dishes that are almost as unhealthy. Still, this Tex Mex chain known for Baby Back Ribs and Big Mouth Burgers has some better-for-you options, too.

Ruby Tuesday

Most Ruby Tuesday restaurants feature a large salad bar, but unfortunately, it contains many high-calorie items. In general, fat and calories are lurking in unexpected places here, so be specific about order requests and alterations to ensure a healthful meal. If you're watching your sodium, exercise caution. Their online nutrition information doesn't include sodium; assume all foods are high in sodium.

Red Lobster

Red Lobster boasts a menu full of lean protein from under the sea. However, the fish, shellfish and seafood here is often batter-dipped and covered in sauces. Luckily there are plenty of grilled and light options, if you know where to look.

PF Chang's

PF Chang's takes Chinese food up a notch. The portions are generous and the combos unique. The chain offers both small and large portions, whole-grain brown rice and sauces on the side to help you create a customized meal. A bit of planning can ensure your special meal is a healthy one!

Outback Steakhouse

This Australia-inspired chain is known for its steaks and the Bloomin' Onion, a deep-fried, batter-dipped appetizer that has more than 2,300 calories! While you'll find plenty of over-the-top dishes, Outback's menu has some healthy fare, too. With a little preparation, you can find a Down Under meal that won't weigh you down.

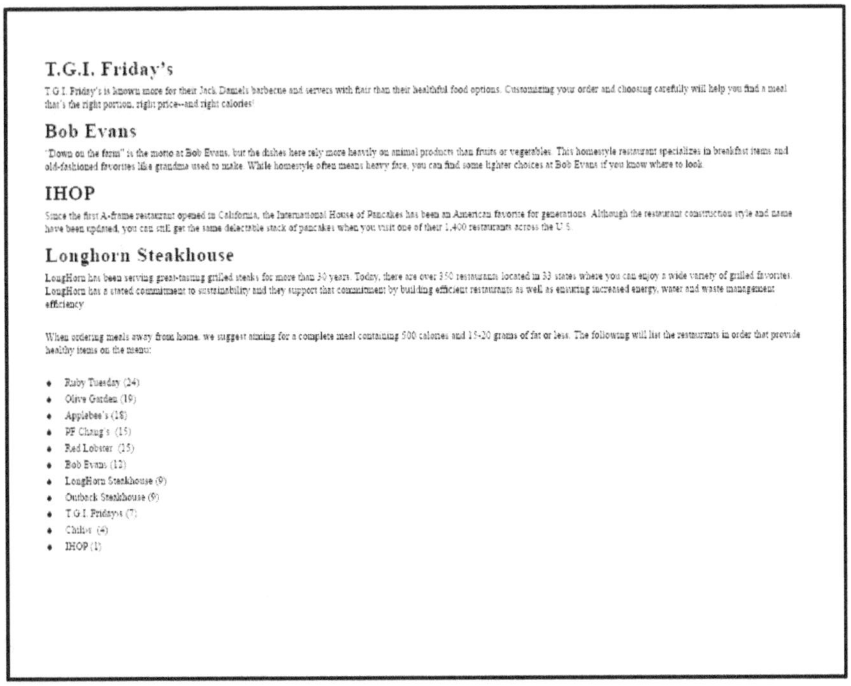

T.G.I. Friday's

T.G.I. Friday's is known more for their Jack Daniels barbecue and servers with flair than their healthful food options. Customizing your order and choosing carefully will help you find a meal that's the right portion, right price--and right calories!

Bob Evans

"Down on the farm" is the motto at Bob Evans, but the dishes here rely more heavily on animal products than fruits or vegetables. This homestyle restaurant specializes in breakfast items and old-fashioned favorites like grandma used to make. While homestyle often means heavy fare, you can find some lighter choices at Bob Evans if you know where to look.

IHOP

Since the first A-frame restaurant opened in California, the International House of Pancakes has been an American favorite for generations. Although the restaurant construction style and name have been updated, you can still get the same delectable stack of pancakes when you visit one of their 1,400 restaurants across the U.S.

Longhorn Steakhouse

LongHorn has been serving great-tasting grilled steaks for more than 30 years. Today, there are over 350 restaurants located in 33 states where you can enjoy a wide variety of grilled favorites. LongHorn has a stated commitment to sustainability and they support that commitment by building efficient restaurants as well as ensuring increased energy, water and waste management efficiency.

When ordering meals away from home, we suggest aiming for a complete meal containing 500 calories and 15-20 grams of fat or less. The following will list the restaurants in order that provide healthy items on the menu:

- Ruby Tuesday (24)
- Olive Garden (19)
- Applebee's (18)
- PF Chang's (15)
- Red Lobster (15)
- Bob Evans (12)
- LongHorn Steakhouse (9)
- Outback Steakhouse (9)
- T.G.I. Friday's (7)
- Chili's (4)
- IHOP (1)

The completed version is called: **C:\Data\InDesignCC-1\Formatting.Indd**

Chapter 5 - Styles Panel

Styles will allow you to change a font or paragraph parameter. All text formatted within the chosen style, will form throughout the entire document.

Chapter Contents:

Section 1: Core Tools

Concept	Explanation / *Command String in italic.*
5.1 Paragraph Styles	This allows you to apply text formatting globally in order to provide a more consistent overall look. It differs from **Character Styles** because **Paragraph Styles** are applied to the entire paragraph at once, not just characters. ***Type Tool→Select text or frame→Window Menu→ Styles→ Paragraph Styles Panel→Create new style ⧉ →Modify Paragraph Settings.***
5.2 Applying Paragraph Styles	***Select text or frame→Window Menu→Styles→Paragraph Styles Panel→Choose the desired style.***
5.3 Character Styles	This allows you to apply multiple attributes to individual text characters (such as font, size, and color). They can be applied to a sentence, word or single character. ***Type Tool→Select text or frame→Window Menu→Styles→ Character Styles Panel→Create new style ⧉ →Modify Character Settings.***
5.4 Track Changes	Once turned on, **Track changes** will keep track of new changes to the text. ***Edit Menu→Edit in Story Editor→Type Menu→Track Changes→Track Changes in current Story.***
Practice Exercise 34 Track Changes	***File Menu→Place→ D3-Restaurants.docx→Type Menu→Track Changes→Track Changes in Current Story.*** *Make a few changes to text in the story.* ***Edit Menu→Edit in Story Editor→Type Menu→Track Changes→Previous/Next/Accept/Reject.***
5.5 Setting Tabs	There are four commonly used tabs: Left-Justified ↓, Centered-Justified ↓, Align-to-Decimal ↓, and Right-Justified ↓. ***Type Menu→Show hidden Characters.*** ***Type Tool→Select text→Type Menu→Tabs→Choose the proper marker to set the tab.***
Practice Exercise 35 Setting Tabs	1. ***File Menu→New→Document→Number of Pages: 2, Portrait, 1 column, Margin: .5 in (3p0)→Ok.*** 2. ***Type Menu→Show Hidden Characters*** 3. ***Type Menu→Tabs*** 4. Type the following and press the **Tab Key** between each word. Note: The » character is the visible tab character. » Name » Department » Wage » Status¶ » Jeff » HR » 50,000.00 » Active¶ » Jane » Engineering » 40,000.0 » Inactive¶ 5. Select the text.

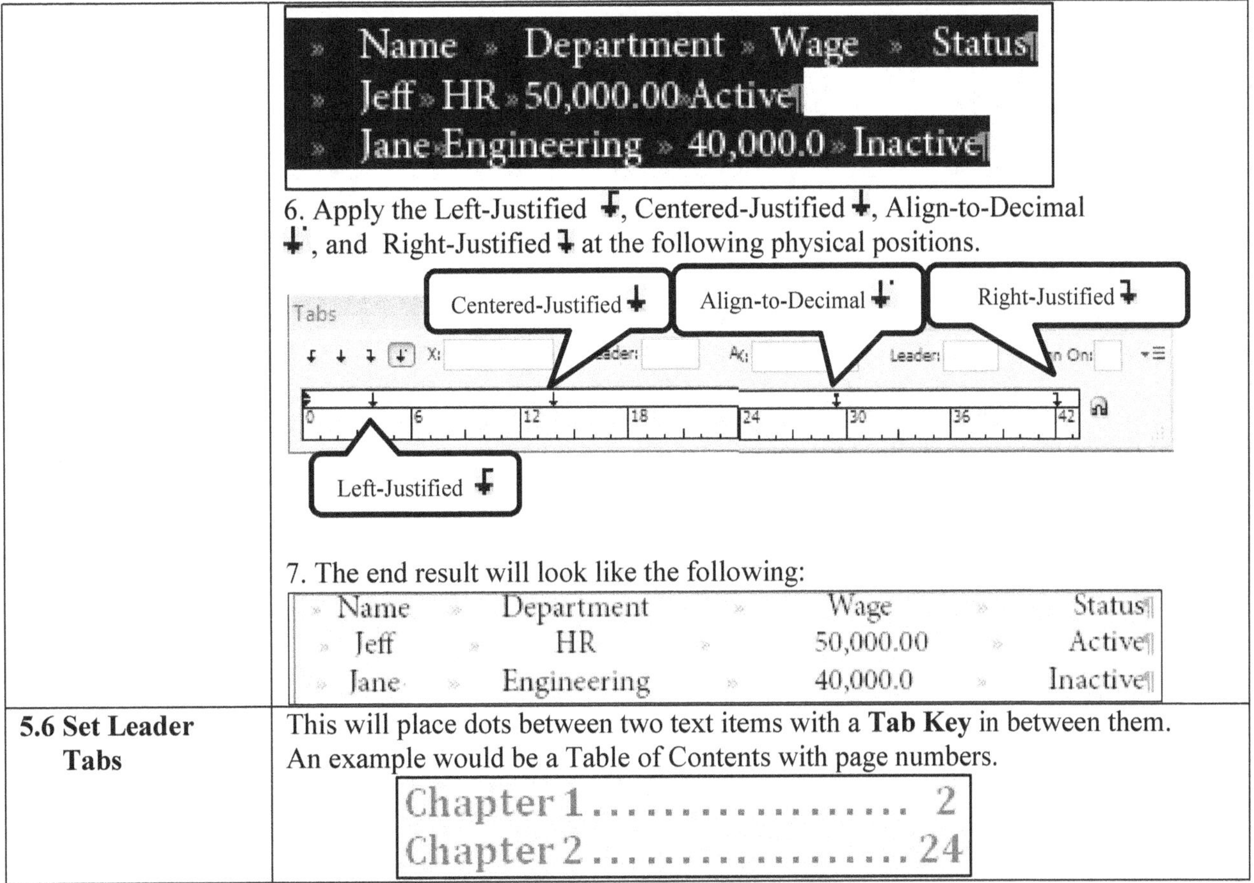

	» Name » Department » Wage » Status¶ » Jeff » HR » 50,000.00»Active¶ » Jane»Engineering » 40,000.0 » Inactive¶ 6. Apply the Left-Justified, Centered-Justified, Align-to-Decimal, and Right-Justified at the following physical positions. Centered-Justified Align-to-Decimal Right-Justified Tabs Left-Justified 7. The end result will look like the following: » Name » Department » Wage » Status¶ » Jeff » HR » 50,000.00 » Active¶ » Jane » Engineering » 40,000.0 » Inactive¶
5.6 Set Leader Tabs	This will place dots between two text items with a **Tab Key** in between them. An example would be a Table of Contents with page numbers. Chapter 1.................. 2 Chapter 2..................24

Practice Exercise 36 *Set Leader tabs*	1. ***File Menu→New→Document→*** ***Portrait, 1 column, Margin: .5 in (3p0)→Ok.*** 2. ***Type Menu→Show Hidden Characters***. 3. ***Type Menu→Tabs.*** 4. Type the following applying a tab between the chapter number and the page number. Example: Chapter Space 1 Tab 5 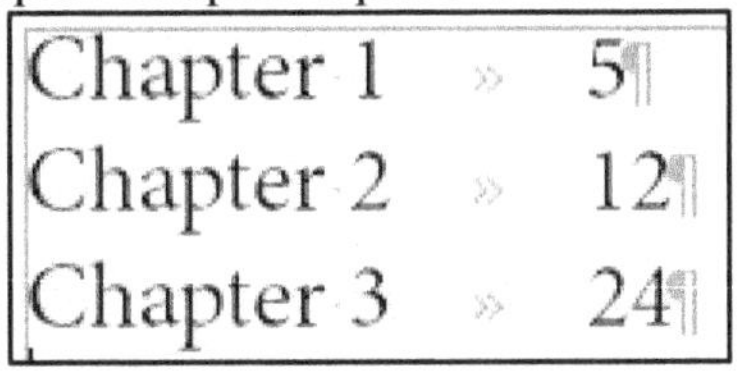 Chapter 1 » 5¶ Chapter 2 » 12¶ Chapter 3 » 24¶ 5. Select the text.  Chapter 1 » 5¶ Chapter 2 » 12¶ Chapter 3 » 24¶ 6. Apply the right tab marker to the selected text and type three dots in the leader box. 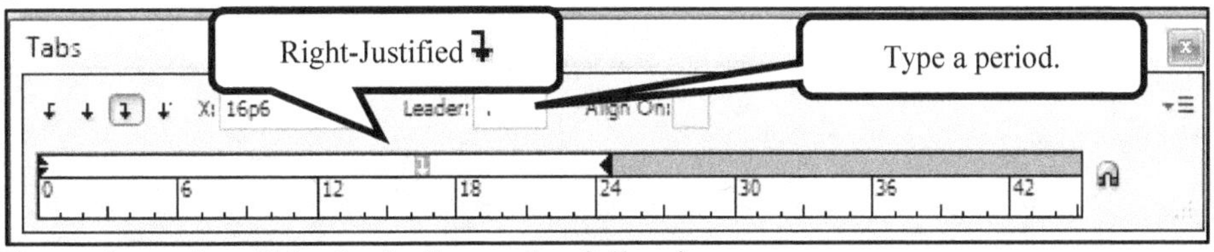 Tabs Right-Justified Type a period. X: 16p6 Leader: . Align On: 0 6 12 18 24 30 36 42 7. The end result will look similar to the following: 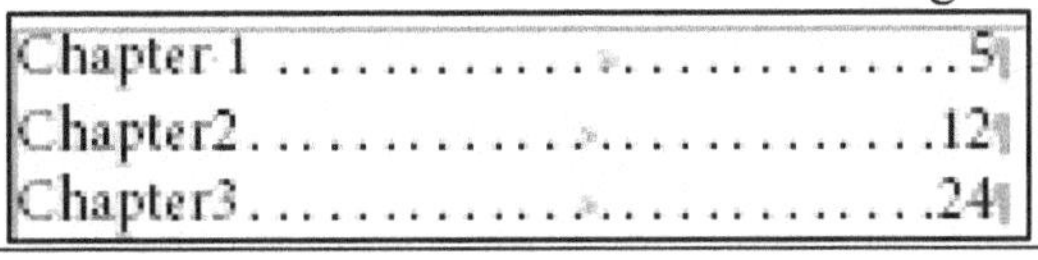 Chapter 1 . . . . .5¶ Chapter2. . . . . .12¶ Chapter3. . . . . .24¶

Section 2: Optional Concepts

Concept	Explanation / *Command String in italic.*
5.7 Applying Character Styles	This will explain how to use **Character Styles**. ***Select text→ Window Menu→Styles→Character Styles Panel→Choose the desired style.***
5.8 Nesting Character Styles	This will allow a **Character Style** to be applied to a **Paragraph Style**. ***Create a Character Style called CC→Create a Paragraph Style called PP→Drop Cap and Nested Styles→New Nested Style→Character Style Name: CC.*** Note: You cannot apply a **Paragraph Style** to a **Character Style**. Note: You can add multiple **Character Styles** to a **Paragraph Style**.
5.9 Object Styles	This will allow you to apply a style to an object or graphic image. ***Select Object→Window Menu→Styles→Paragraph Styles Panel→Create new style →Modify Object Style Settings.***
5.10 Applying Paragraph Styles	This will explain how to use **Paragraph Styles**. ***Select Object→ Window Menu→Object Styles Panel→Choose the desired style.***
5.11 Nesting Object Styles	This will allow you to nest one style as the master style. It can then be used in other styles. *Create an Object style:* ***AA→Create new style****: BB* ***→General Tab→Based on: AA.***
5.12 Table Styles	This will allow you to apply a style to a table. *Select Table→* ***Window Menu→Styles→Table Styles Panel→Create new style →Modify Table Style Settings.***
5.13 Applying Table Styles	This will explain how to use table styles. ***Select Table→Window Menu→ Table Styles Panel→Choose the desired style.***
5.14 Nesting Table Styles	This will allow you to nest one table style as the master style. Then, it can also be used as a master style in other styles. ***Window Menu→Styles→ Table Styles Panel→Create new style: AA→ Create new style****: BB* ***→General tab→Based on: AA.***
5.15 Globally Updating Styles	If you make any changes to a child style, the parent style will be updated.
5.16 Local Formatting	Local formatting will block the nested styles to be applied. A Plus (+) sign will appear if the nested style cannot be applied.
5.17 Redefine	When there is a **plus (+)** sign displayed, it indicates that local formatting is preventing the style to be applied. The **Redefine Tool** will apply the local text format to all text formatted in the style.
5.18 Clear Over-Ride	When there is a **plus (+)** sign displayed, it indicates that local formatting is preventing the style to be applied. **Clear Over-Ride** will force the local text to use the defined style, or over-ride the local formatting.
5.19 Loading Styles from External Program	When you import a Word document, you will inherit its styles. ***File Menu→Place→ Show Import Options→*** Import Styles Automatically Paragraph Style Conflicts: Auto Rename Character Style Conflicts: Auto Rename

Chapter 6 - Long Document Elements

Here, we will create the elements needed to support a long document.

Chapter Contents:

Section 1: Simple Table Of Contents

Student Project D - Simple Table Of Contents

Concept	Explanation / *Command String in italic.*
6.1 Book Structure	A book structure allows you to create a separate file for each chapter and views it as an entire book. Page numbers and other elements will be adjusted properly. ***File Menu→New→Book.***
6.2 Sync Documents	This is the function that verifies and assures that everything in the book structure is correct. ***Book Panel→Menu*** ***→Sync selected documents***.
Student Project D-1 Creating a Book	1. ***File Menu→New→Document→****[Default]* ***→Ok.*** *File menu→****Save as****→ Name: TOC.****innd****.* 2. ***File Menu→New→Document→****[Default]* ***→Ok.*** *File menu→****Save as****→ Name:* ***Section1.innd****.* 3. ***File Menu→New→Document→****[Default]* ***→Ok.*** *File menu→****Save as****→ Name:* ***Section2.innd****.* 4. ***File Menu→New→Book→****Name:* ***Book Master→Save*** *Add all documents by pressing the button and put them in the proper order.*  5. Add additional pages to the Section 1 document. Double click on Section 1 document→Pages Panel→Create new page Icon → Create new page Icon 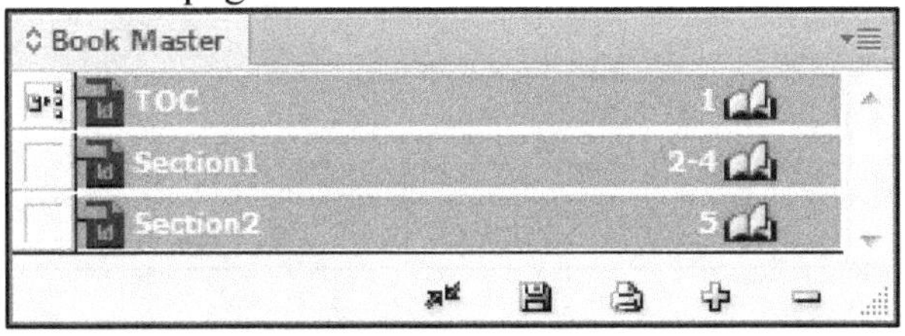 . 6. Sync documents if necessary
6.3 Table of Contents	A Table of Contents is created from defined styles, but it can also be applied to a book structure. ***Layout Menu→Table of Contents***.
Student Project D-2 Table of Contents	Continue from previous practice exercise. 1. **Open TOC Document** Create a Paragraph style: ***Window Menu→Styles→Paragraph Styles***. Paragraph Style: **Heading1** Based on: Basic Paragraph (18pts, Arial, Bold,) Paragraph Style: **TOC Title** (Based on: Basic Paragraph, 36pts, Arial, Bold) Paragraph Style: **TOC Heading1** (Based on: Basic Paragraph, 24pts, Arial, Bold) Sync Paragraph styles: Select all documents→Sync

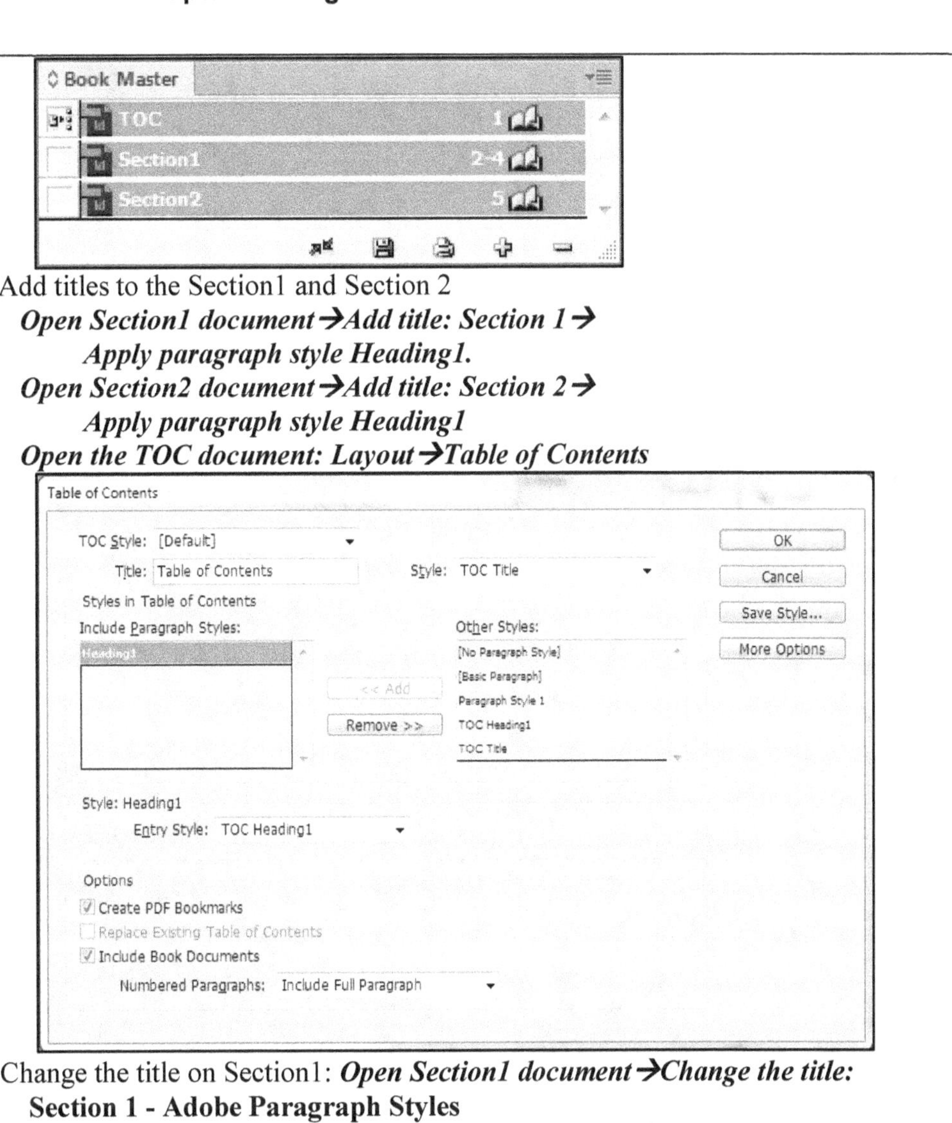

Add titles to the Section1 and Section 2

Open Section1 document→Add title: Section 1→ Apply paragraph style Heading1.

Open Section2 document→Add title: Section 2→ Apply paragraph style Heading1

Open the TOC document: Layout→Table of Contents

Change the title on Section1: ***Open Section1 document→Change the title:*** **Section 1 - Adobe Paragraph Styles**

Change the title on Section2: ***Open Section2 document→Change the title:*** **Section 2 - Adobe Character Styles**

Update the Table of Contents: ***Open TOC Document→Layout→Update Table of Contents.***

Add leaders to Table of contents:

Open TOC Document→Select Section1 and Section2 titles→Type→Tabs→Select the right-Justified tab and add it to 42 on the ruler→Add a dot to the leader box.

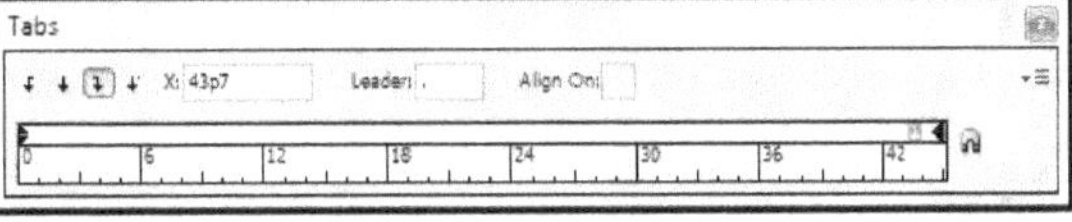

The end result will look similar to the following:

Table Of Contents

Section 1 - Adobe Paragraph Styles............. 4

Section 2 - Adobe Character Styles............. 5

Student Project E - Comprehensive Table Of Contents

This is a comprehensive exercise to cover chapters, sub-chapters, odd/even pages, page numbers, iii page numbers, tabs, leaders, index, and footnotes.

Section 2: Comprehensive Table Of Contents

Student Project E-1 *Creating* *Table of Contents*	All documents should be saved in folder ***C:\Data\InDesignCC-All.*** 1. **Create Title Document** ***File Menu→New→Document (8-1/2X11, 1 Pages, 1 columns)→***OK. Paragraph Style: **Heading1 Based on: Basic Paragraph (18pts, Arial, Bold,)** Paragraph Style: **Heading2 (Based on: Basic Paragraph, 14pts, Arial, Bold)** Paragraph Style: **TOC Title (Based on: Basic Paragraph, 36pts, Arial, Bold)** Paragraph Style: **TOC Heading1** **(Based on: Basic Paragraph, 24pts, Arial, Bold)** Paragraph Style: **TOC Heading2 (Based on: Basic Paragraph, 20pts, Arial, Bold, Left Indent=.5 in)** Page 1-Title=**InDesign Documentation, 36 Points, Center, Bold→**Ok. ***File Menu→Save as→TitlePage.indd→Save→File Menu→Close*** 2. **Create Introduction** ***File Menu→New→Document*** *(8-1/2X11, 3 Pages, 1 columns, Facing Pages)* ***File Menu→Save as→Introduction.indd→Save→File Menu→Close*** 3. **Create Chapter 1** ***File Menu→New→Document (8-1/2X11, 3 Pages, 1 columns, Facing Pages)*** ***File Menu→Save as→Chapter1.indd→Save→File Menu→Close.*** 4. **Create Chapter 2** ***File Menu→New→Document (8-1/2X11, 3 Pages, 1 columns, Facing Pages)*** ***File Menu→Save as→Chapter2.indd→Save→File Menu→Close.*** 5. **Create Book and synchronize styles** ***File Menu→New→****Book* ***→MyNewBook.indb*** ***Add Document ✣ →TitlePage.indd*** ***Add Document ✣ →Introduction.indd*** ***Add Document ✣ →Chapter1.indd*** ***Add Document ✣ →Chapter2.indd*** Note: Notice that all documents contain the paragraph styles. ***Select all documents→More Options →Synchronize Book→OK*** 6. **Add content to Chapters** **Introduction.indd** First Page of a document: **Page 1** - Leave Blank, This is where the Table of Contents will be placed. **Page 2** -Title=**Introduction**, Heading1 (Labeled as Page 3). **Page 3** - Subtitle=**CopyRights**, Heading2 **Page 3** - Text=**All rights reserved**, Basic Paragraph, Character Style=None, 12pts, Courier New ***File Menu→Save*** **Chapter1.indd** **Page 1** - Title=**Chapter 1** (Heading1) (Labeled as Page 5) **Page 2** - Subtitle= **Section 1.1** (Heading2) **Page 3** - Subtitle= **Section 1.2** (Heading2) ***File Menu→Save*** **Chapter2.indd** **Page 1** - Title=**Chapter 2** (Heading1) **Page 2** - Subtitle= **Section 2.1** (Heading2)

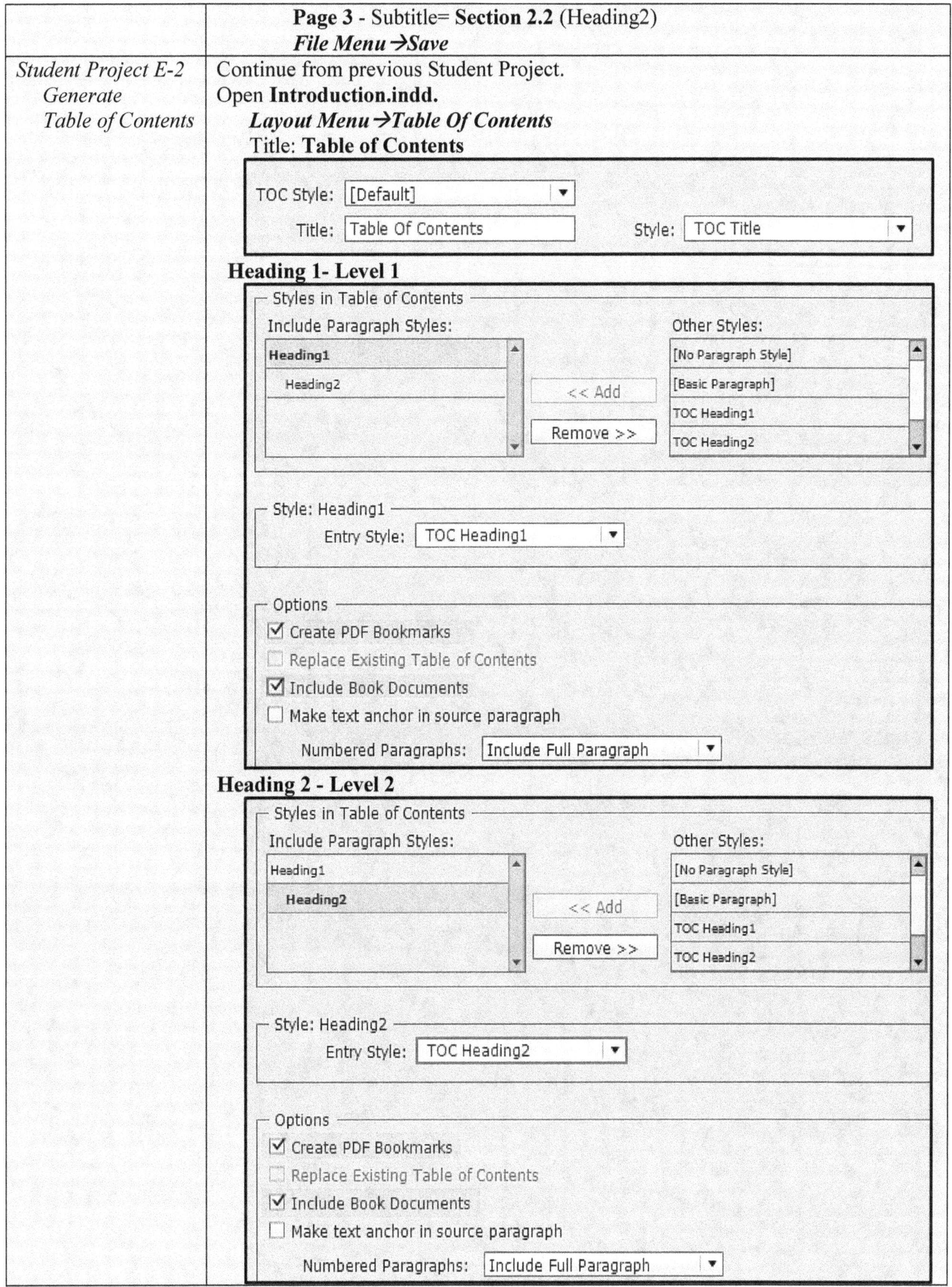

	Page 3 - Subtitle= **Section 2.2** (Heading2) ***File Menu →Save***
Student Project E-2 *Generate* *Table of Contents*	Continue from previous Student Project. Open **Introduction.indd.** ***Layout Menu →Table Of Contents*** Title: **Table of Contents** TOC Style: [Default] Title: Table Of Contents Style: TOC Title **Heading 1- Level 1** Styles in Table of Contents Include Paragraph Styles: Heading1, Heading2 << Add Remove >> Other Styles: [No Paragraph Style], [Basic Paragraph], TOC Heading1, TOC Heading2 Style: Heading1 Entry Style: TOC Heading1 Options ☑ Create PDF Bookmarks ☐ Replace Existing Table of Contents ☑ Include Book Documents ☐ Make text anchor in source paragraph Numbered Paragraphs: Include Full Paragraph **Heading 2 - Level 2** Styles in Table of Contents Include Paragraph Styles: Heading1, Heading2 << Add Remove >> Other Styles: [No Paragraph Style], [Basic Paragraph], TOC Heading1, TOC Heading2 Style: Heading2 Entry Style: TOC Heading2 Options ☑ Create PDF Bookmarks ☐ Replace Existing Table of Contents ☑ Include Book Documents ☐ Make text anchor in source paragraph Numbered Paragraphs: Include Full Paragraph

	OK→Place the Table of Contents on Introduction Page 1. **The end result will look similar to the following:** **Table Of Contents** Introduction 2 Copy Rights 2 Chapter 1 5 Section 1.1 6 Section 1.2 7 Chapter 2 8 Section 2.1 9 Section 2.2 10
6.4 Odd or Even Page	When printed, a blank page will be inserted to force an even or odd page.
Student Project E-3 Set Odd or Even Page	Continue from previous Student Project. **Start chapter on an odd or even page.** To set up each chapter on Odd pages, do the following: ***Select Introduction→Book Panel More Options*** → ***Book Page Numbering*** *Options* **Continue on Next Odd Pages →OK.** Options Page Order: Continue from previous document Continue on next odd page Continue on next even page Insert Blank Page Automatically Update Page & Section Numbers Note: Each chapter will now start on an odd page.
6.5 Add Page Numbers	This will add page numbers.
Student Project E-4 Add Page Numbers to the Footer	Continue from previous Student Project. Perform the following on **Introduction, Chapter1, and Chapter2.** Add Page numbers to the footer of the Master Pages. Create Text box at the bottom of the page and type the word "Page " ***Type Menu→Insert Special Character→Markers→Current Page Number*** **Format it to be Arial, 24pts, and Bold.** Add to all pages.
6.6 Introduction to be iii	Set Introduction to ii.

Student Project E-5 Set Introduction to ii	Continue from previous Student Project. **Set Introduction to be iii and Chapters to be 123 numbering style** Open Introduction: ***Book→More Options*** ***→Document Numbering Options.*** *Note: CS5 use:* ***Book→More Options*** ***→Numbering and Section Options.*** 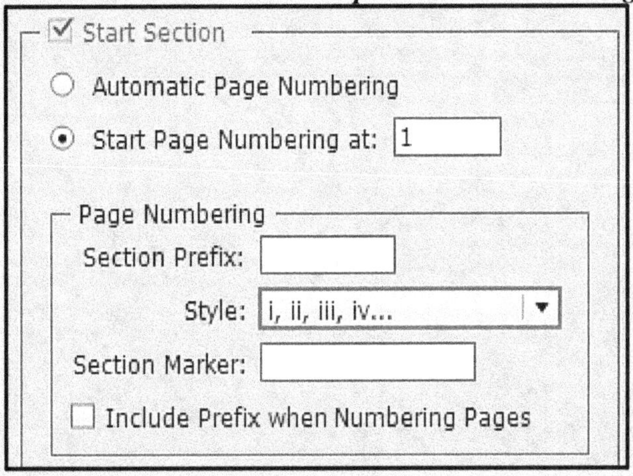 Start Section Automatic Page Numbering Start Page Numbering at: 1 Page Numbering Section Prefix: Style: i, ii, iii, iv... Section Marker: Include Prefix when Numbering Pages Open Chapter 1 ***Book→More Options*** ***→Document Numbering Options*** 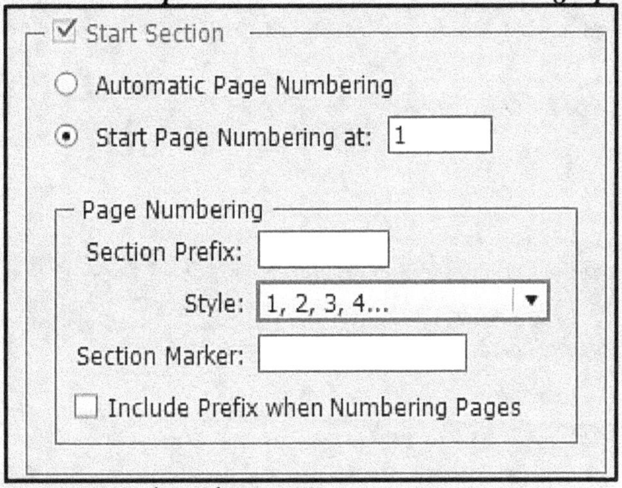 Start Section Automatic Page Numbering Start Page Numbering at: 1 Page Numbering Section Prefix: Style: 1, 2, 3, 4... Section Marker: Include Prefix when Numbering Pages Page structure end results: 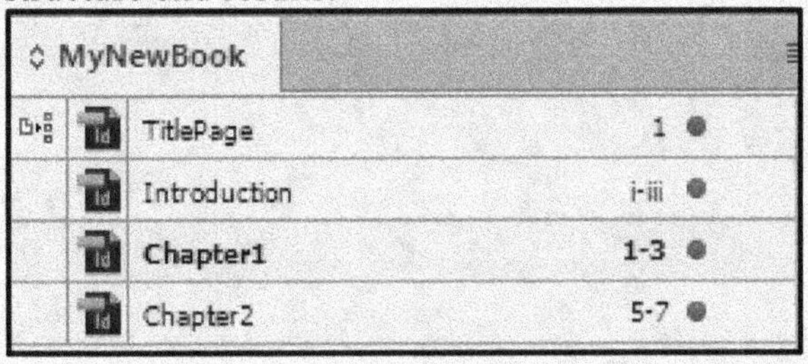 MyNewBook TitlePage 1 Introduction i-iii **Chapter1 1-3** Chapter2 5-7 Update Table Of Contents: ***Layout Menu→Update Table Of Contents.***
6.7 Set up the Tabs	This will set up the tabbing.

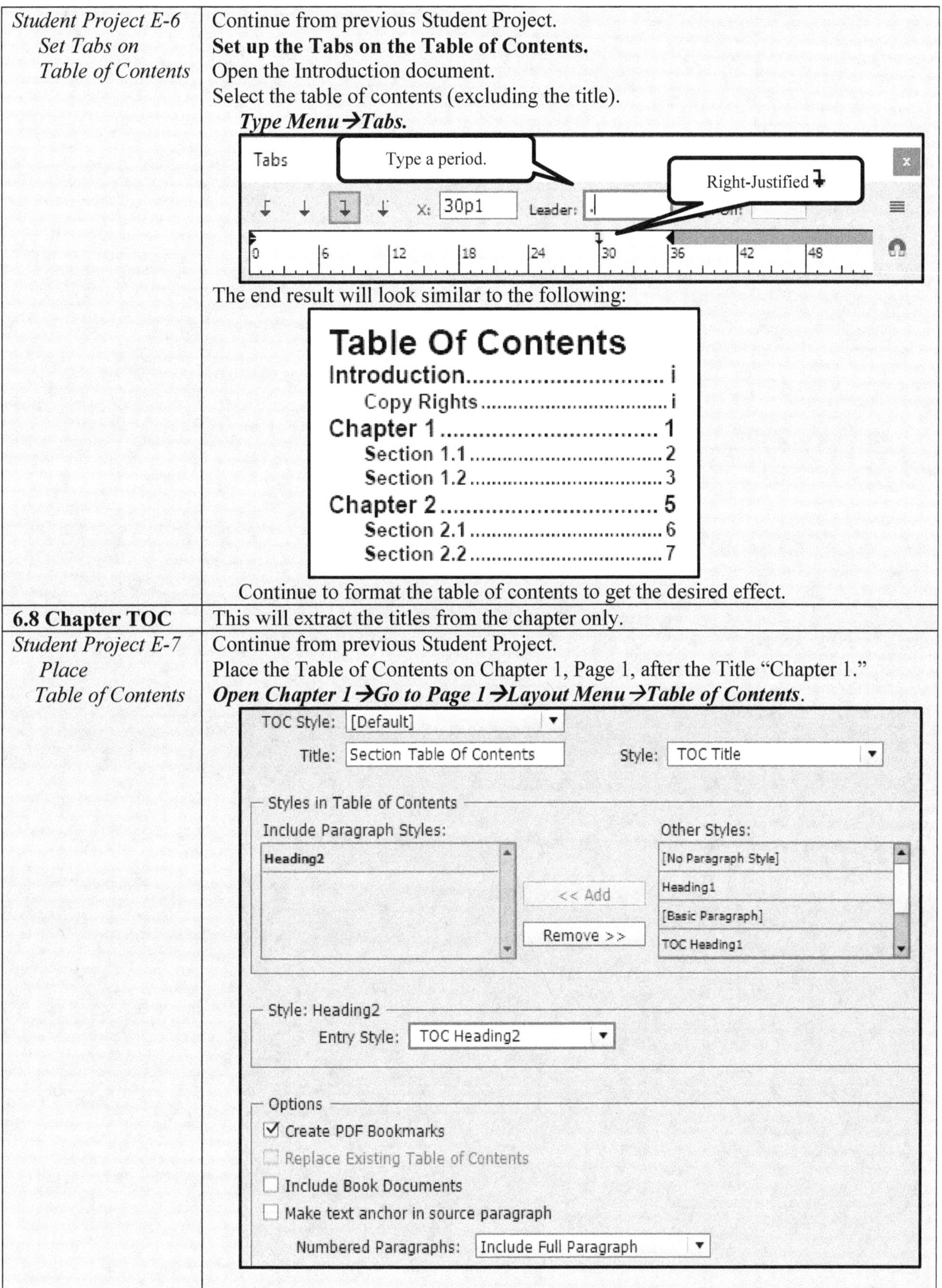

Student Project E-6 *Set Tabs on* *Table of Contents*	Continue from previous Student Project. **Set up the Tabs on the Table of Contents.** Open the Introduction document. Select the table of contents (excluding the title). ***Type Menu→Tabs.*** The end result will look similar to the following: **Table Of Contents** **Introduction** .... i Copy Rights .... i **Chapter 1** .... 1 Section 1.1 .... 2 Section 1.2 .... 3 **Chapter 2** .... 5 Section 2.1 .... 6 Section 2.2 .... 7 Continue to format the table of contents to get the desired effect.
6.8 Chapter TOC	This will extract the titles from the chapter only.
Student Project E-7 *Place* *Table of Contents*	Continue from previous Student Project. Place the Table of Contents on Chapter 1, Page 1, after the Title "Chapter 1." ***Open Chapter 1→Go to Page 1→Layout Menu→Table of Contents.***

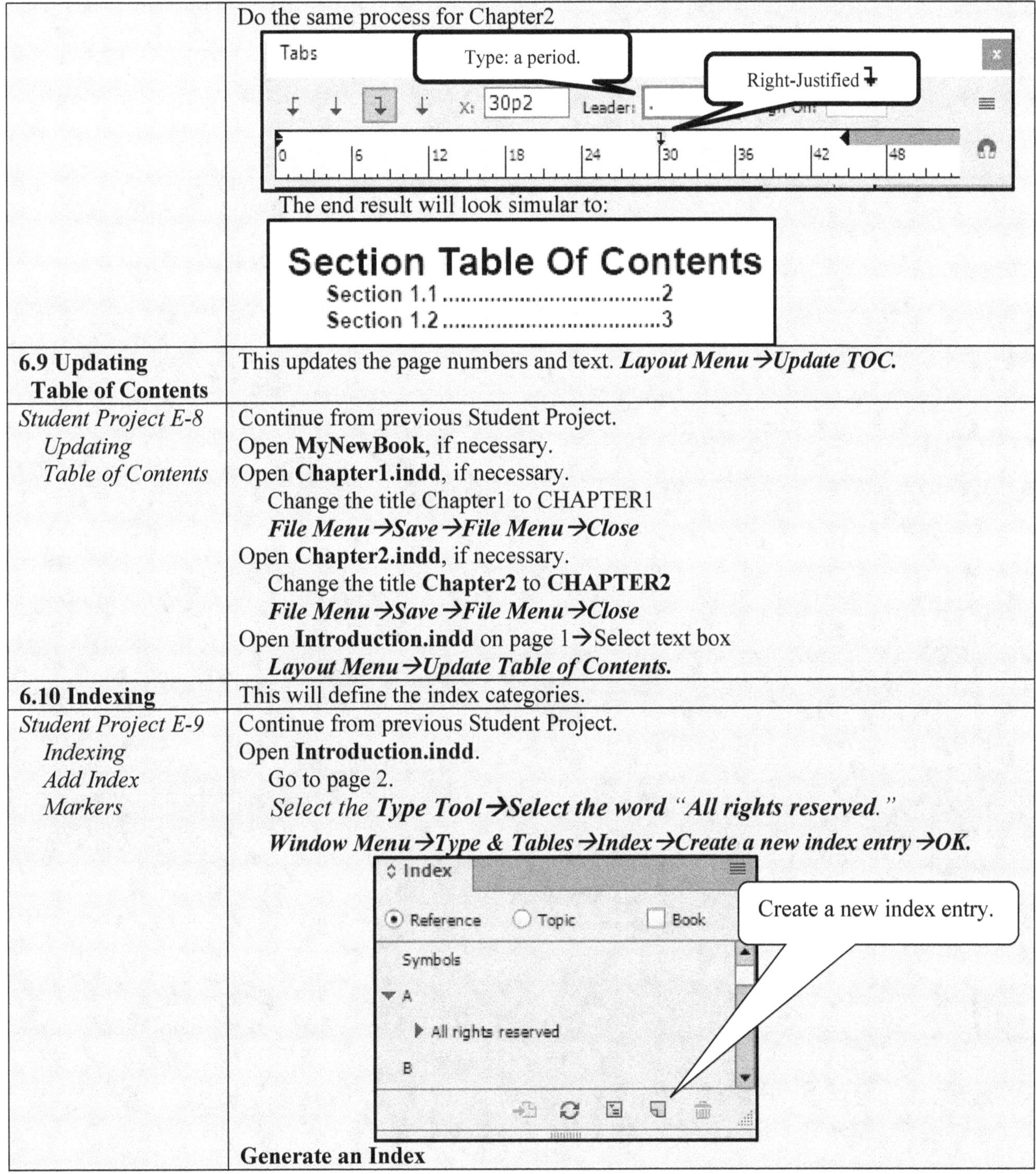

	Do the same process for Chapter2 Type: a period. Right-Justified The end result will look simular to: **Section Table Of Contents** Section 1.1 ....2 Section 1.2 3
6.9 Updating Table of Contents	This updates the page numbers and text. ***Layout Menu→Update TOC.***
Student Project E-8 Updating Table of Contents	Continue from previous Student Project. Open **MyNewBook**, if necessary. Open **Chapter1.indd**, if necessary. Change the title Chapter1 to CHAPTER1 ***File Menu→Save→File Menu→Close*** Open **Chapter2.indd**, if necessary. Change the title **Chapter2** to **CHAPTER2** ***File Menu→Save→File Menu→Close*** Open **Introduction.indd** on page 1→Select text box ***Layout Menu→Update Table of Contents.***
6.10 Indexing	This will define the index categories.
Student Project E-9 Indexing Add Index Markers	Continue from previous Student Project. Open **Introduction.indd**. Go to page 2. *Select the **Type Tool→Select the word "All rights reserved."*** ***Window Menu→Type & Tables→Index→Create a new index entry→OK.*** Create a new index entry. **Generate an Index**

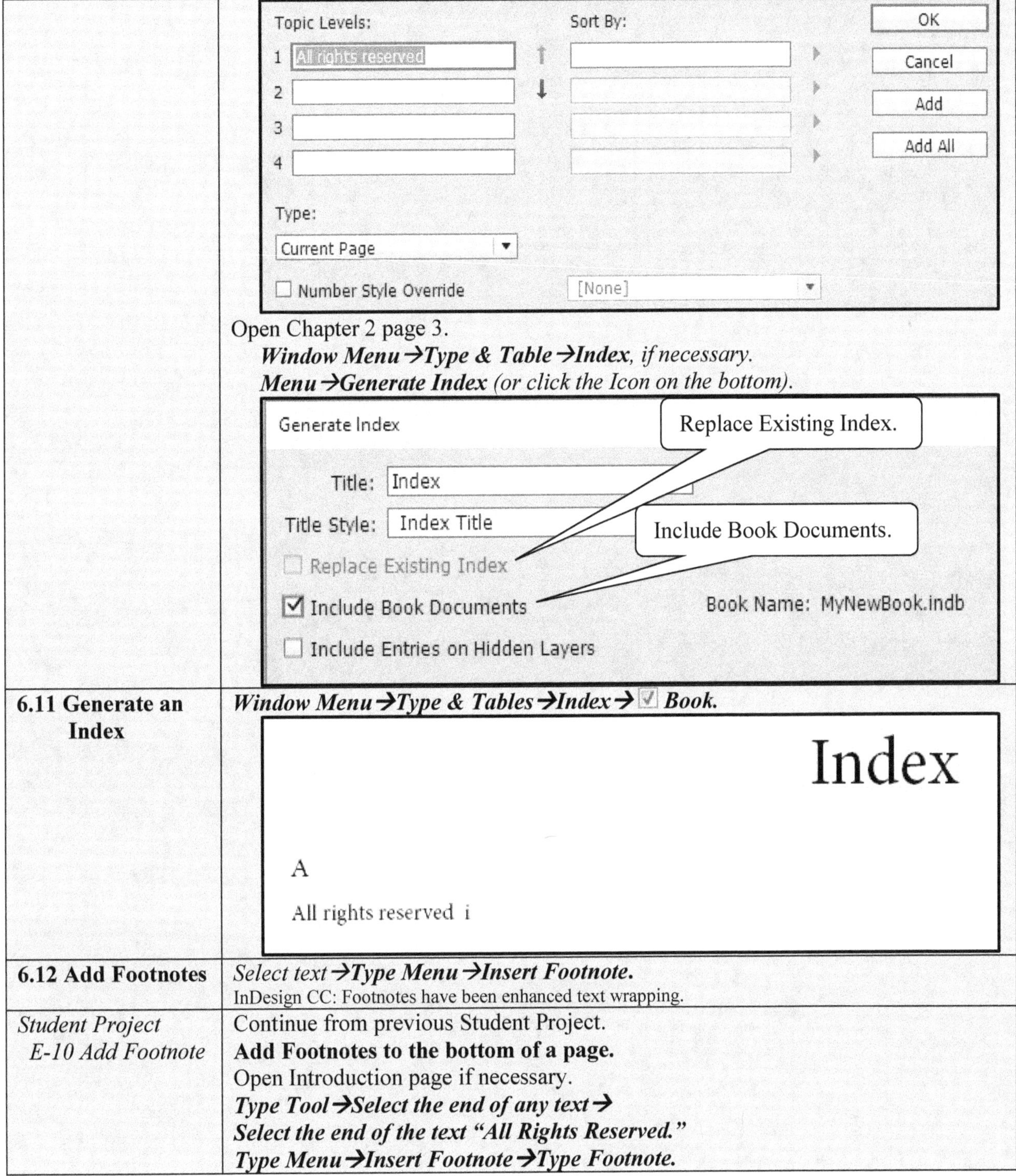

	Open Chapter 2 page 3. ***Window Menu→Type & Table→Index**, if necessary.* ***Menu→Generate Index** (or click the Icon on the bottom).*
6.11 Generate an Index	***Window Menu→Type & Tables→Index→☑ Book.***
6.12 Add Footnotes	*Select text→**Type Menu→Insert Footnote.*** InDesign CC: Footnotes have been enhanced text wrapping.
Student Project E-10 Add Footnote	Continue from previous Student Project. **Add Footnotes to the bottom of a page.** Open Introduction page if necessary. ***Type Tool→Select the end of any text→*** ***Select the end of the text "All Rights Reserved."*** ***Type Menu→Insert Footnote→Type Footnote.***

Chapter 7 - Import / Export And Print

When finished, there are several export capabilities.

Chapter Contents:

Section 1: Export

Concept	Explanation / *Command String in italic.*
7.1 Package Files	Packages link objects into one folder in order to transport projects. ***File Menu→ Package→Review Warnings→Package→Folder name.***
7.2 Merged Data	This is similar to mail merge in Microsoft Word.

Section 2: Optional Concepts

7.3 Layer Comps	This a way to build different layouts in order to view different possibilities. However, this must be done in **Photoshop** in order to link the **Photoshop** file: ***Object Menu→Object Layer Options.***
7.4 EPUB eBooks	InDesign CC+: This creates the industry standard EPUB for eBooks. ***File Menu→Export→Name: Test→Save as Type: EPUB.***
7.5 QR Code	InDesign CC+: This creates a QR Code. ***Object Menu→Generate QR Code→Type: Web Hyperlink→URL:*** www.excel-networks.com
7.6 Export to PDF	***File Menu→Export→Save as type: Adobe PDF (interactive)→Save button.*** **Interactive** - This includes elements such as movies, hyperlinks, bookmarks, and buttons. **Print** - This does not contain any interactivity.
7.7 PDF Pass-Through Printing	You can print directly to a PDF print engine rather than exporting. The print quality is the same as Exporting. ***File Menu→Print→Printer: Adobe PDF→ Output Menu on the right→Color: Composite Leave Unchanged→Print button.***
7.8 TrueType Fonts	**TrueType Fonts** can be scaled to any size and are clear and readable in all sizes. They can be sent to any printer or other output device supported by Windows. Cambria Sample; Cambria Math Sample. TrueType fonts are indicated by a T in the font name (***Type Menu→Font***).
7.9 OpenType Fonts	**OpenType Fonts** provide a greater character set range, such as small capitalization, old-style numerals, and more detailed shapes, such as glyph and ligatures. **OpenType Fonts** can be sent to any printer or other output device supported by Windows. Calibri Sample; Californian FB Sample. OpenType fonts are indicated by an O in the font name (***Type Menu→ Font***).
7.10 Download Fonts	To download additional fonts to InDesign: 1. Go to a website that lists downloadable **TrueType** or **OpenType Fonts.** Such as: http://www.1001fonts.com/opentype-fonts.html 2. Fonts are usually contained in a Zip folder. Un-compress the file and place the files in a temporary folder. 3. ***Right-Click on the TrueType (.ttf) or OpenType (.otf) file→Install*** 4. To view the installed file: ***Start→Control Panel→Fonts folder.***

Practice Exercise 38	Open the file in the Zip Utility and install to the font library. *Browse Disk:* ***Start Button→Computer/Browse disk→ C:\Data\InDesignCC-All folder.*** *Open Zip:* ***Right-Click→Open with WinZip→space-age.zip.*** *Uncompress Zip file:* ***Select the file to unzip→UnZip/Share Tab→ UnZip.*** *Install Font:* ***Locate the file on the disk (extension .ttf or .otf)→Right-Click→ Install.*** *Verify Installation:* ***Check InDesign to see if it has been installed (Type Menu→ Font).***

Student Project F - Olympic Newsletter

If time permits, students can work on individual projects.
These projects will involve creating a newsletter, including text and graphics of the 2006 Winter Olympics. Please don't spend a lot of time reading and matching the articles and pictures. The primary purpose is to put together an InDesign structure using as many features as possible. Feel free to use any feature you have learned in the class and any other feature that would enhance your presentation.

The following are some suggestions for creating your base outline:

1. Create a preset page called "Olympic Template."
2. Create an **A-Master** page on a standard **8-1/2 x 11** layout with header/footer adding the author, title and page number on the two spreads.
3. Create a **B-Master** and rename it to "**B-2 Column Text**." Use the guides to layout the master page and link it to the **A-Master** page.
4. Create a **C-Master** and rename it to "**C-1 Column Text**." Use the guides to layout the master page and link it to the **A-Master** page.
5. Create a **D-Master** and rename it to "**D-Text With Graphics**." Use the guides to layout the master page and link it to the **A-Master** page.
6. Create multiple pages in the Pages Panel with the master pages previously designed.
7. Place some text on the pages using **Manual**, **Semi-Auto** and **Automatic** text placement techniques.
8. Place some graphics images in between columns of text using the **Text Wrap** pane and create a graphic picture page with labels under the pictures.
9. Add **stroke** (borders) around some of the graphic images.
10. Reshape some of the text frames at an angle.
11. Use **anchor points** to reshape some of the graphic images.
12. Place a **quote** (with large/centered text) in the middle of a page.
13. Rotate some text as a side label on the graphic placement page such as "**2006 Winter Olympics.**"
14. Convert some of the graphic image frames to an **ellipse**, **triangle**, or **polygon** shape.

    Documents to use:

    Article1-Figure Skating Outfits Lacking Style.docx
    Article2-Olympics on TV Where's the buzz.docx
    Article3-The Olympic Emotion of the Opening Ceremony.docx
    Article4-Failing anti-doping test.docx
    Article5-Flag Bearers for the Opening Ceremony.docx
    Article6-Sasha Cohen took the ice.docx
    Article7-Sasha Cohen Falls Twice.docx

    Graphic Files to use:

Student Project I - Olympic Newsletter

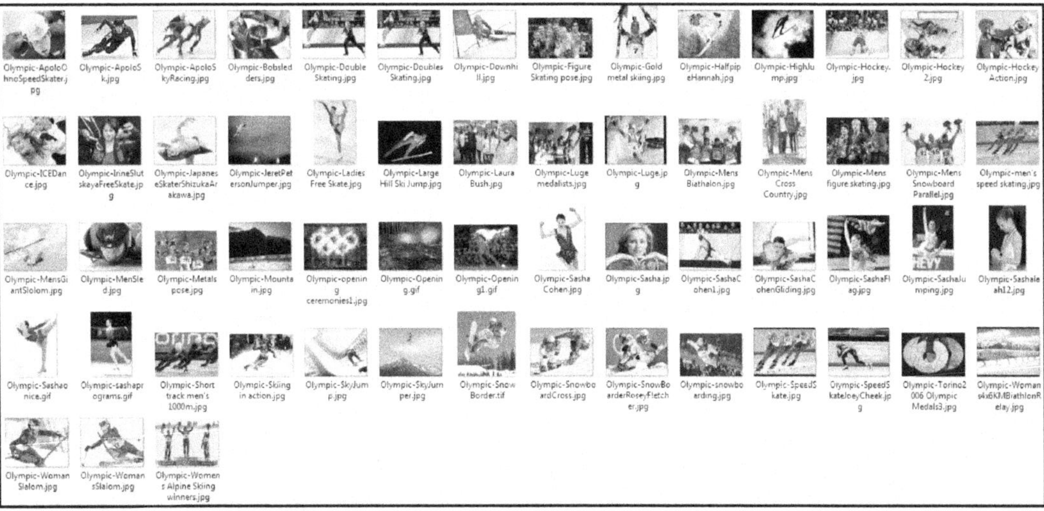

Optional Graphic images: Download the files from the following Olympic websites:

www.olympic.org or www.london2012.com or http://www.teamusa.org

Front Cover

2012 Olympic Soccer: US Women's Hopes for Four-Peat in Rio Rely on Alex Morgan

Alex Morgan's assist to Carli Lloyd in the eighth minute of their game against Japan helped the U.S. Olympic women's soccer team take an early lead and win the gold medal for the third straight time.

The 2012 Olympics were the first for Morgan, and she left her mark on London, scoring three times and playing a vital role in the Americans' gold medal run.

While the Americans found a winning combination again this year, they will lose quite a few key members of the team for the next Games.

Hope Solo will be 35 and could be done, along with backup goalkeeper Nicole Barnhart, who will be 34. Abby Wambach will be 36 and in the final stages of her career, if she is still around. The hero of this year's gold medal game, Carli Lloyd, will be 34 and aging, and several other members may be gone or too old to be effective.

The team needs new leaders.

Among the young women who will be around and trying to lead the U.S. to a four-peat for gold in the 2016 Rio Games will be Morgan, the focal point of the team's offense.

Apart from being tied for fifth in scoring in this year's Olympics, Morgan already owns a big role with the U.S. squad. The *Orlando Sentinel* has called her the X-factor, while *USA Today* already referred to her as "the star of U.S. women's soccer."

Morgan scored 16 goals in her first 32 games with the national team, and has been a constant source of offense.

According to the *USA Today* article, she played well when forced to change her role in the gold medal game, and she has become a very versatile player.

When the Olympics roll around again in four years, Morgan will be the clear leader of the team. She is the future for U.S. soccer, and the hope for a fourth straight gold will rely on her.

Morgan helped lift the team to an extra time win over Canada this year, and in Rio she will try to take another step and lead the Americans to yet another gold.

Back Page

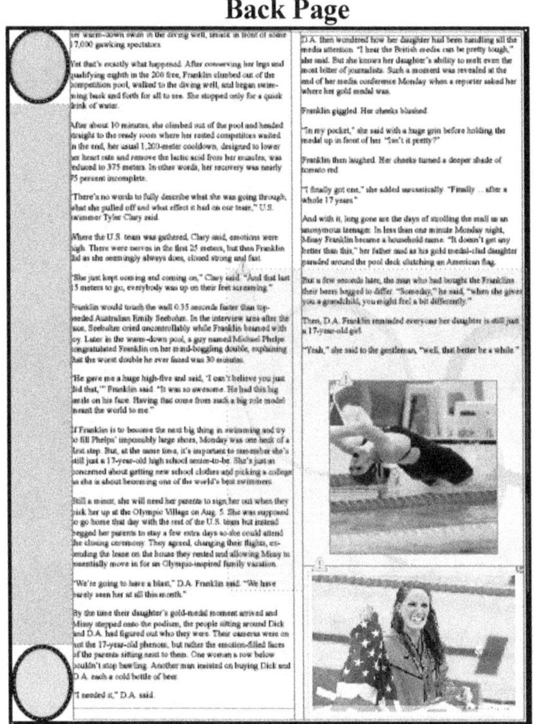

her warm-down swim in the diving well, smack in front of some 17,000 gawking spectators.

Yet that's exactly what happened. After conserving her legs and qualifying eighth in the 200 free, Franklin climbed out of the competition pool, walked to the diving well, and began swimming back and forth for all to see. She stopped only for a quick drink of water.

After about 10 minutes, she climbed out of the pool and headed straight to the ready room where her rested competitors waited. In the end, her usual 1,200-meter cooldown, designed to lower her heart rate and remove the lactic acid from her muscles, was reduced to 375 meters. In other words, her recovery was nearly 75 percent incomplete.

"There's no words to fully describe what she was going through, what she pulled off and what effect it had on our team," U.S. swimmer Tyler Clary said.

Where the U.S. team was gathered, Clary said, emotions were high. There were nerves in the first 25 meters, but then Franklin did as she seemingly always does, closed strong and fast.

"She just kept coming and coming on," Clary said. "And that last 15 meters to go, everybody was up on their feet screaming."

Franklin would touch the wall 0.35 seconds faster than top-seeded Australian Emily Seebohm. In the interview area after the race, Seebohm cried uncontrollably while Franklin beamed with joy. Later in the warm-down pool, a guy named Michael Phelps congratulated Franklin on her mind-boggling double, explaining that the worst double he ever faced was 30 minutes.

"He gave me a huge high-five and said, 'I can't believe you just did that,'" Franklin said. "It was so awesome. He had this big smile on his face. Having that come from such a big role model meant the world to me."

If Franklin is to become the next big thing in swimming and try to fill Phelps' impossibly large shoes, Monday was one heck of a first step. But, at the same time, it's important to remember she's still just a 17-year-old high school senior-to-be. She's just as concerned about getting new school clothes and picking a college as she is about becoming one of the world's best swimmers.

Still a minor, she will need her parents to sign her out when they pick her up at the Olympic Village on Aug. 5. She was supposed to go home that day with the rest of the U.S. team but instead begged her parents to stay a few extra days so she could attend the closing ceremony. They agreed, changing their flights, extending the lease on the house they rented and allowing Missy to essentially move in for an Olympic-inspired family vacation.

"We're going to have a blast," D.A. Franklin said. "We have barely seen her at all this month."

By the time their daughter's gold-medal moment arrived and Missy stepped onto the podium, the people sitting around Dick and D.A. had figured out who they were. Their cameras were on not the 17-year-old phenom, but rather the emotion-filled faces of the parents sitting next to them. One woman a row below couldn't stop bawling. Another man insisted on buying Dick and D.A. each a cold bottle of beer.

"I needed it," D.A. said.

D.A. then wondered how her daughter had been handling all the media attention. "I hear the British media can be pretty tough," she said. But she knows her daughter's ability to melt even the most bitter of journalists. Such a moment was revealed at the end of her media conference Monday when a reporter asked her where her gold medal was.

Franklin giggled. Her cheeks blushed.

"In my pocket," she said with a huge grin before holding the medal up in front of her. "Isn't it pretty?"

Franklin then laughed. Her cheeks turned a deeper shade of tomato red.

"I finally got one," she added sarcastically. "Finally ... after a whole 17 years."

And with it, long gone are the days of strolling the mall as an anonymous teenager. In less than one minute Monday night, Missy Franklin became a household name. "It doesn't get any better than this," her father said as his gold medal-clad daughter paraded around the pool deck clutching an American flag.

But a few seconds later, the man who had bought the Franklins their beers begged to differ. "Someday," he said, "when she gives you a grandchild, you might feel a bit differently."

Then, D.A. Franklin reminded everyone her daughter is still just a 17-year-old girl.

"Yeah," she said to the gentleman, "well, that better be a while."

Center Foldout

London Summer Games 2012

Kerri Walsh, Misty May-Treanor Win Olympic Gold Medal In Beach Volleyball (PHOTOS)

LONDON — Misty May-Treanor danced on the sand and then off it, leaving Horse Guards Parade with Kerri Walsh Jennings and a third gold medal.

Playing in the Summer Games together for the last time, the twice-defending champions extended their unbeaten streak to 21 in a row – through Athens, Beijing and now London – by defeating Jennifer Kessy and April Ross 21-16, 21-16 in an all-American final on Wednesday night.

The match started with nearby Big Ben pealing the hour and ended with the "Star-Spangled Banner" rising from the iconic venue in the Prime Minister's backyard, just down the Mall from the royal residence at Buckingham Palace. Playing on Henry VIII's former jousting tiltyard, with the current Prince Harry in the crowd, Walsh Jennings and May-Treanor continued their reign as champions of the beach.

"It's insane. It doesn't feel like it's real," Walsh Jennings said. "I told Misty when we were getting our medals: 'If I wake up tomorrow and we have to replay this match, I'm going to be furious.' Because it feels like I'm in a dream.

"It truly feels surreal and it didn't feel like that the first two times for whatever reason. But this, it's almost too good to be true."

Dominating the sport for three Olympiads, Walsh Jennings and May-Treanor have won every match they've ever played at the Summer Games and lost just one of 43 sets.

No one had ever won even two beach volleyball gold medals before the Americans won their second straight in Beijing.

No woman had ever won three Olympic beach volleyball medals of any kind.

"I know how hard it is to win one tournament. And the amount of tournaments they've won is crazy," said Kessy, who jumped for joy on the medal podium after she and Ross won silver in their Olympic debuts. "For them to do it for years and years and to be on top is just really impressive. We learn a lot from them."

Earlier Wednesday, Brazil's Juliana and Larissa beat Xue Chen and Zhang Xi of China to win the bronze.

Brazil's Emanuel and Alison were scheduled to play Julius Brink and Jonas Reckermann of Germany in the men's gold-medal match on Thursday night. Martins Plavins and Janis Smedins of Latvia were to play Reinder Nummerdor and Rich Schuil of the Netherlands for the men's bronze.

Walsh Jennings and May-Treanor pulled away midway through the first set of the title match and were never threatened in the second, falling to their knees and hugging as Ross' serve went long on match point. Then they took the celebration to the stands, circling the stadium that was built on the 500-year-old parade grounds now used by the Queen's household cavalry.

Walsh Jennings covered her bare shoulders with an American flag and grabbed her children; the older one was a little scared. They high-fived the Horse Guards Parade Dance Team and volunteers and just about anyone holding an American flag.

And, with both teams in the final from the United States, there were a lot of them.

"It's one thing to play an Olympic final. It's another to play against a team from your county you know so well," said Walsh Jennings, who played with Kessy on a U.S. junior team.

"I think the only reason Misty and I are gold medalists is because of those two. They push us so hard. They're one of my favorite teams to beat because they're so good. They've been one of the top teams in the world since they got together. I'm just really grateful that we've had them to come up against because they've made a big difference in our career."

May-Treanor returned to the sand for a funky jig to rival the scantily clad dance team that helped bring the beach party atmosphere to the sold-out crowds in central London.

"I was like, 'I hope I'm not rubbing it in anybody's face,' but I was so excited," said May-Treanor, a competitor on "Dancing with the Stars" in 2008 before she tore her left Achilles tendon in rehearsal and missed a year on the pro tour. "I just had to get out there and let it out."

May-Treanor said she will retire to raise a family with her husband, Los Angeles Dodgers catcher Matt Treanor, who watched the gold-medal match in the team's clubhouse on a balky Internet connection that made him miss the final few points.

"I'm just real proud of her," he said in the Dodger Stadium dugout. "I am sure she is much more comfortable on the court than I am watching her."

During the medal ceremony, the four Americans hugged after receiving their prizes and stood facing the two American flags raised during the national anthem. Despite both a shutout in the men's tournament, the United States matched its best finish since beach volleyball was added to the Olympics in 1996.

"I'm happy to be sitting next to another American team up here," May-Treanor said. "For both of us to be in the gold-medal match, it says a lot about our sport, a lot about the teams up here. ... I'm proud about both of us. And I'm just happy about the four of us really sharing this moment. They have no reason to hang their heads down."

Franklin blossoms into champion

LONDON -- D.A. Franklin was busy talking, trying to put into words what it feels like to watch your bubbly, affectionate 17-year-old daughter win at the Olympics. That's when her husband, Dick, tapped her on the shoulder and interrupted.

"Honey," he said. "Your daughter is about to get her gold medal."

From that moment on, Dick and D.A. Franklin didn't speak. There were no words. They just sat there and watched, tears streaming down their cheeks as they tried to absorb this mind-blowing moment. Their little girl, the one who never wanted to get out of the water, the one who was the first one to swim in the lake outside their home on a frigid March morning, had blossomed into an Olympic champion.

They had sworn they never cared about a gold medal, that their love for their little girl would be the same whether she won at the Olympics or came in last. But now the feeling was overwhelming. It didn't seem real. Not their daughter who still comes home from swim practice exhausted, climbs into the leather recliner with her father and falls asleep on his chest.

*Quinn Rooney/Getty Images*Missy Franklin's 100-meter backstroke win was her first Olympic gold and second overall medal of the London Olympics.

Certainly not in the 100-meter backstroke, far from her best event. And definitely not in the fourth-fastest time ever.

"I need somebody to pinch me," D.A. said.

On the podium down below, Missy Franklin needed the same. Although she had controlled her emotions throughout her chaotic night, she was struggling now. She tried to sing the national anthem through the tears but had so many thoughts racing through her head that she admitted she forgot the words. The red, white and blue flag rising to the rafters also tugged at her heart.

"That flag was so unbelievable," she said later. "I never dreamed it would be like that."

No one could have dreamed her night would have gone like this. As far back as a year ago, Franklin and her coach, Todd Schmitz, knew this night could be a challenge with Franklin potentially swimming in the 200 freestyle semifinals on the same night as the 100 back final. But never did they imagine she would have a mere 14 minutes between the two races.

Never did they think the Aquatics Centre would be set up in such a way that it would be a seven-minute walk to the warm-down pool and USA Swimming would have to ask for special permission for Franklin to do

Index - InDesign CC Beyond The Basics

www.ingramcontent.com/pod-product-compliance
Lightning Source LLC
Chambersburg PA
CBHW082216220526
45470CB00010B/3190

* 9 7 8 1 9 7 6 4 6 7 0 0 4 *